# CITROËN 2CV

## THE COMPLETE STORY

# Other Titles in the Crowood AutoClassics Series

# CITROËN 2CV

## THE COMPLETE STORY

MATT WHITE

THE CROWOOD PRESS

First published in 1999 by
The Crowood Press Ltd
Ramsbury, Marlborough
Wiltshire SN8 2HR

**www.crowood.com**

Paperback edition 2005

**British Library Cataloguing-in-
Publication Data**
A catalogue record for this book is available
from the British Library.

ISBN 1 86126 731 2

**Dedication**
To Ken Smith

Typeface used: New Century Schoolbook.

Typeset and designed by
D & N Publishing
Lowesden Business Park
Lambourn Woodlands
Hungerford, Berkshire.

Printed and bound by CPI Bath.

**Acknowledgements**

A large number of people have made a terrific
contribution towards making this book possible
by providing photographs and other archive
material, scale models or cars for photography
and by being interviewed. Ken Smith, ex-Chief
Engineer at Citroën in Slough gave me such help
that I could not have contemplated the job without him. His archive material and photographs
set the scene for this book. The National Motor
Museum at Beaulieu has provided a large part of
the photographic archive but so has the 2CV
Club of Great Britain through the help of its
archive officer Alan Cofflard.

Graham Draper of Garage Levallois also provided many unique archive photographs and was
very helpful providing technical advice on how to
run a 2CV today. He also made his workshop
facilities available and provided cars for photography. David Conway of the Citroën Car Club
imparted his unique knowledge of the scale
model world and made his massive collection of
models available for photography. Martin Woodley of the 2CV Racing Club gave me a great
insight into the racing scene and motoring scribe
and photographer Phil Llewellin gave his excellent report and photographs of the Mondello 2CV
24 hours race. Friend and colleague James Taylor also gave help and advice as well as masses of
material to make my job easier.

Thanks also to Maurice Rowe for providing his
original photographs and to Sarah Ellis for making her 'rhubarb and custard' 2CV all clean and
tidy for photography.

*Classic Cars* magazine and staff also provided
me with the excuse for investigating the story of
the 2CV in the first place for an article in 1995
and was responsible for giving me the enthusiasm to start such a project as a whole book. With
their help and encouragement my writing skills
progressed from merely being a humble Club
magazine editor to a writer of books.

# Contents

## Evolution of the 2CV

| | |
|---|---|
| 1936 | Pierre Boulanger, newly appointed managing director of Citroën – unveils his design brief for the toute petit voiture, the simple, utilitarian car for the masses. |
| 1937 | The first prototype, assembled by André Lefèbvre's team, is tested at the La Ferté-Vidame track. |
| 1938 | Twenty prototypes are made for testing and are of various types. |
| 1939 | The final prototype is submitted for appraisal fitted with the water-cooled engine and torsion bar suspension. Two-hundred and fifty pre-production TPVs are made for appearance at that year's Paris Salon show. War is declared on 3 September and the show is cancelled. |
| 1940 | The 250 cars are hidden when Germany invades France. Later most of them were destroyed. |
| 1941–45 | Secretly Boulanger continues development of the new car and recruits Walter Becchia to design an air-cooled, two-cylinder engine. |
| 1946–48 | Development continues and culminates in the appearance of the new 2CV at the Paris Salon on 7 October 1948. |
| 1949 | Production of the Type A saloon 2CV commences in July. |
| 1951 | The Fourgonnette AU van is launched in France. |
| 1953 | Citroën's factory in Slough, England, builds a right-hand-drive version of the 2CV, complete with metal bootlid which is to be adopted universally by 1957. |
| 1954 | A new 425cc engine is offered alongside the original 375cc unit. |
| 1958 | The four-wheel-drive, twin-engined Sahara is launched. |
| 1960 | The archaic multi-ribbed bonnet is replaced by a smoothed down five-rib version |
| 1960 | Fibreglass Bijou, based on the 2CV is produced by the Slough factory. |
| 1961 | Ami-6 derivative is launched in France. |
| 1964 | Production of 2CVs at Slough ceases. |
| 1965 | Bodywork of the 2CV is updated with a new six-light design complete with front-hinged front doors. |
| 1967 | Dyane introduced with 425cc engine. |
| 1970 | New engines complement the 2CV range with 435cc and 602cc types being offered. |
| 1974 | 370,512 examples of 2CVs of all types were produced in this year. |
| 1980 | A new lease of life for the 2CV arrives in the shape of the popular Charleston special edition. |
| 1988 | Nearly 3.5 million 2CVs had been produced at the Levallois factory outside Paris by the time it closed this year. |
| 1990 | The last manufacturing base of the 2CV since the closure of Levallois, is at Mangualde in Portugal, where in July this year the last 2CV of all is completed. |

# Introduction

The fog that shrouded Paris in late 1948 permeated deep into Citroën's Quai de Javel headquarters after the launch of the new Deux Chevaux. The press was almost unanimous in its scorn of the new design: 'Do you supply the can opener with it?' asked an American journalist, while *The Autocar* commented, 'The designer has kissed the lash of austerity with almost masochistic fervour.'

But the Paris Motor Show of 1948 brought one and a quarter million visitors to the Citroën stand who thought differently. The French farmers – for whom, partly, this economical car was designed – liked what they saw and thousands of orders were placed at the Show for a car that would not arrive for another year.

What the journalists had failed to notice was that the new Citroën 2CV had five winning characteristics: simplicity, reliability, ingenuity, cheapness to buy and an appealing vitality that made it the car for kings as well as commoners. Later, when the 2CV became available as assembled in Slough from 1953, *The Motor* described it rather more kindly as a 'vehicle with almost every virtue except speed, silence and good looks'.

My introduction to the 2CV happened in the late 1970s, when a photographer I assisted lent me his to run all sorts of errands. After a few miles of getting used to the 'push me, pull you' gearchange, I slowly appreciated the characteristic gait of 2CV driving: rev hard in every gear, try to maintain progress whenever possible and never use fourth unless you can see a mirage in the arrow-straight road ahead! I became quite proficient at driving this quirky little car around London. I took some pains to try to unstick the tyres, but the alarming rate of body roll seemed to control adhesion very well. In a way, I think the roll scared the driver into slowing down.

To see my employer drive this Citroën he'd had for years was amazing. The control, the relaxed but very fast progress and his habit of speeding up to sixty whenever there were 6ft 6in restrictions to negotiate earned him credibility points in my eyes. The unmitigated thrashing that the car took appeared never to bother it. Minor bits and pieces fell off it now and again, but it always kept on going and almost every weekend went haring off to deepest Herefordshire at breakneck speed. However, it was only while researching an article for *Classic Cars* magazine that I discovered the amazing story behind the 2CV.

But for the Second World War, the Deux Chevaux might have appeared nine years earlier. In the mid-1930s Pierre Boulanger, then Managing Director of Citroën, had put an idea to his Chief Engineer, Maurice Broglie, for a revolutionary vehicle that would have some rather specialized specifications. It must be a four-wheeled car capable of carrying two peasants and 50kg of potatoes at a speed of 60km/h, and must return an economy of 3ltr × 100km. It must also be able to be driven on terrible roads: Boulanger's words were, 'If a box of eggs were placed in the car and it was driven over a ploughed field, not a single egg would be broken.'

During the winter of 1937 several pre-production prototypes were tested at a secret location at Ferté-Vidame on a test track built under the supervision of Boulanger himself. These prototypes were made with aluminium body panels, corrugated for strength, and with a semi-monocoque construction. The engine was a water-cooled flat twin with twin carburettors. Optimum weight for the entire package was to be 300kg. With testing more or less complete by spring 1938, Pierre Boulanger was happy enough to order 250 to be made for the following year's Salon and for sending to dealers.

After some tantalizing hints to the press about the new baby, all seemed set for the launch when international events took control. Pierre Boulanger, as a supporter of de Gaulle, was determined not to let the TVP – the *Toute Voiture Petite* as the project was then called – into the hands of the occupying Germans. Most of the Salon cars were ordered to be scrapped, while a few were secreted here and there. It is quite likely that, despite Boulanger's best efforts, one example did find its way into German possession.

The factory was put over to building trucks by 1942. Boulanger recruited Walter Becchia from Talbot to redesign the engine in secret as an air-cooled unit, and arranged for the body and platform to be remade in steel under the direction of Jean Cadiou. The somewhat unsatisfactory torsion-bar suspension was replaced by an innovative, centrally located coil spring for each side of the car. The twin-carburettor induction system gave way to a single carb and the air-cooled design overcame the potential problems of running the water-cooled version in conditions of extreme cold.

By the end of the war most of the technicalities of the project had been ironed out, but problems in the supply of materials and goodwill from the government meant that Renault was able to get its Volkswagen-inspired 4CV into production first, by 1947.

So we come to the beginning of our story, with the unveiling in 1948 of the car that was to mobilize rural France, to shrug off the scorn of the early press reports and push its way through to 1990, when the last example was made at Citroën's Mangualde factory in Portugal. The Deux Chevaux has been manufactured or assembled from kits in twenty countries, with many local variations according to demand. The fact that it survived so long is probably an acute embarrassment to Citroën itself, whose market placing has since gone up in the world. The fact that these 'tin snails' are as popular as ever doesn't help the firm, the new products of which might just possibly lack comparable charm.

# 1  André Citroën

André Citroën, son of a Dutch-Jewish diamond merchant who had set up business in Paris, was born in 1878 at 44 Rue Lafitte in the 9th *arrondisement*. His father, Levie Citroën, was from Amsterdam and had taken French nationality in 1871, settling in Paris with his Polish-Jewish wife, Masza. The couple were to have five children: Bernard, Hugues, Fernande and Jeanne, André being the youngest. He went to school at the Lycée Condorcet where he was to meet a future competitor, Louis Renault, and in 1898 earned himself a place at the élite Ecole Polytechnique. André's mother died suddenly in 1899 at the age of forty-six, and he joined the French Army as an engineering officer in 1900.

Early in 1900 André went to Poland on holiday with his sister Jeanne, who had married a wealthy Polish banker in Warsaw. On an excursion to Glówno, an industrial town between Lodz and Warsaw, he met a distant relation who ran an engineering factory. The works included a foundry where mechanical parts and gears were made in the traditional way with sand-box moulds made from wooden dies. Here he noticed a reduction gear set of a most unusual design: the teeth were cut with a V shape running down the centre of the perimeter of each gear wheel. The type was ideally suited to the transmission of heavy gear loads. Obviously of a helical design due to the angle of the V, the gears ran very quietly and created no axial thrust, and were self centring.

Bearings to support the gear sets would take no more than rotational loads rather than end thrust as in most single helical gears. To ensure a perfect mesh, the accuracy of the teeth had to be high – it presented an intriguing engineering problem.

*André Citroën.*

The usual method would be to cast the gear and grind the teeth to profile later, but the precision required could not be gained by this method. The only other option was to cut the grooves from a cast or forged blank disc of high-quality tool steel. The task is difficult enough with straight or single helical teeth, but the V shape made it much harder. Yet, on a small scale this factory had managed to do it. At the time the technique was well in advance of the skills of large-scale engineering companies in Europe, if not the world.

Outside Europe, in America particularly, developments in metallurgy and mechanical engineering were rapidly progressing and André Citroën was well aware of the future possibilities of the new discoveries. New steels had been put to use in lathe tools and a super-hard chrome-steel type had been demonstrated in Paris which could cut through case-hardened steel with ease.

## BIRTH OF THE COMPANY

The thought occurred to Citroën that, armed with the inspired idea of the Polish factory and the application of the new American metal manufacturing processes, he could produce the new gears and set himself up in business. He persuaded his sister's banker husband, Bronislaus Goldfeder, to finance the deal and Citroën bought the patent and licence for the idea on the same day. Together with André Boas and Jacques Hinstin – two friends from the Lycée Condorcet– he set up a workshop and offices at the Faubourg Saint-Denis to perfect the manufacture of the unique double chevron or double helical gears. The type was to be described both ways by Citroën in advertising.

The engineering itself was not without problems. The major stumbling block was the small radius change of direction at the centre of each gear tooth. The normal procedure would be to make two separate cuts for each side of the tooth, leaving a fettling problem at the centre, or to have each side of the gear tooth unconnected in two halves, which would compromise the strength and integrity of the design. Citroën realised that with the new technology becoming available, the preferred and indeed mechanically demanded solution – a machine which could cut each tooth with one uninterrupted stroke of a high-speed revolving tool – was possible.

He devised an end-milling machine which, when fitted with a tool made of the new chrome-steel, could cut each gear tooth to a perfectly profiled shape ready for use. The great leaps forward in manufacturing technology of the period meant that Citroën could put his new 'invention' to good use in a marketplace crying out for reduction gears able to withstand high speeds and massive loads, and still run silently.

Most manufacturing processes of the time were beginning to turn from steam or water power – essentially slow running sources of power – to that provided by electric motors that, in order to provide the large amounts of power required, had to run fast and have the take-off of power transmitted through a suitably robust reduction gear, down to a workable speed: enter the Citroën patented double chevron gear system which was to provide André Citroën with the enduring symbol of the Citroën empire up to the present day.

While the gear-making business was very successful, it was never a volume production operation. Gear sets were generally made to the customer's specification for often unique applications. It is said that Citroën's double helical gears were fitted to the steering machinery of the White Star liners *Titanic, Olympic* and *Britannic*. At the top of the rudder stock of such large ships was fitted a geared quadrant driven by a pinion

– itself driven by a small electric or steam motor – meshed together using double helical gears. This was the perfect application for a gear set able to withstand the immense forces bearing on a liner's rudder.

Luckily for Citroën, the range of suitable applications, liners apart, was massive and the solid background of a successful, if small, business gave him the confidence and reputation to attract new business opportunities. His acumen for production methods gained him a valuable contract with the Mors company to streamline its motor car production. And so André Citroën came into contact with the motor car for the first time.

Marrying Georgina Bingen in the spring of 1914, the Citroëns' happiness was to be short-lived. Germany declared war in August and, as a reservist, André was summoned to appear for military duty at once. One of the pitiful and desperate factors of war is that one or often both protagonists are not in the least prepared for such a conflict, either with men, arms or the infrastructure required to fuel the conflict. Citroën at once noticed that the artillery units were under-supplied in ammunition. He quickly realized that France could fall within months when its meagre stocks of shells were exhausted. He drew up plans to produce shells on production lines and, with his reputation a distinct advantage, gained official approval for his scheme.

In March 1915 Citroën purchased thirty acres of old market gardens on the Quai de Javel on the left bank of the Seine within sight of the Eiffel Tower. Using his knowledge of American production methods Citroën planned the factory to mass produce the product with the minimum of manpower and space. Within three months the factory was completed – a model of the simple steel-framed building with applied facades, and in itself a modern solution to be much emulated in the 1920s and 1930s. This may be compared with the Firestone tyre factory on the Great West Road in London, now sadly demolished (the gates remain), a paragon of Art Deco design only bettered in London by the Hoover building at Perivale: it is said that from plans being approved and a bare site to the first tyre being produced at the Firestone factory was only five weeks.

In Paris, only a year after he bought the market gardens, Citroën was producing 10,000 shells per day at Quai de Javel. By the end of the war the factory was producing many times that. One could suggest that the only winners in war are the armaments manufacturers, and the war years certainly did no harm to the standing and reputation of André Citroën.

## THE FIRST CITROËN CARS

The first motor car manufacturers evolved from a background of bicycle- or coach-building in small, labour-intensive, specialized workshops. Joseph Starley in England, for instance, began producing bicycles in Coventry in the 1880s and developed the first 'safety' bicycle, which the company named 'The Rover'. From these small beginnings the Rover Company developed as a low-volume producer of high quality motor cars. Nearly destroyed by the Depression, it was only the timely intervention of the Wilks brothers in 1934 which saved Rover and revolutionized its manufacturing processes. The Rover Company holds the record for the longest unbroken single ownership line in the 'family tree' of British motor manufacturers.

The advent of the first Citroën motor car turned all this pedigree history on its head. His large factory at Quai de Javel could easily have produced any other mass-produced consumer product, but André Citroën chose the motor car as the latest thing in personal

*1921 Type A Torpedo – an early 10hp four-seater.*

travel for those post-war years. From the out-set his factory was designed on mass-production principles in the Henry Ford tradition. He was, of course, determined that the first car he produced would be the best he could make and, quite unusually for the time, it was to be complete and fully fitted-out, ready for the road, when it left the production lines.

The first Citroën, the Type A, was a 1,327cc 8CV with a four-cylinder side-valve engine capable of propelling the car at 40mph. Designed by one of Citroën's former colleagues in the Army Technical Service, Jules Salomon, the Type A was Citroën's idea of the car for every man. Simply constructed of rugged and economical design,

*The 1922 B2 preserved by the Egeskov Veteranmuseum in Denmark. The simple styling and boxy design found favour: by the end of 1922, more than 300 B2s were coming off the production line daily.*

*The early 1920s and B2 models are taking shape at Quai de Javel. Holes are being drilled in the second car to affix the bonnet and engine cowls, as on the leading car. Power for the electric drill is taken from overhead power lines. In the right background, workers – many of them women – observe the photographer. Hanging on hooks nearby are many berets. In the far left distance, engine bulkheads are stacked ready for fitting.*

the Type A was mostly conventional but did incorporate the individualistic detachable cylinder head – perhaps the first hint that the public could expect innovative design from Citroën in the future.

Originally available in convertible 'torpedo style', the body design cleverly allowed for later, different styles to be added to the range. Car buyers would soon be able to choose from five body types: three- and four-seater torpedos; a three-seater saloon; a coupe de ville and a light delivery van. Already Citroën was determined that his cars should appeal to all classes of society, from chauffeur-driven individuals to shop owners and delivery drivers. Available at first at a bargain price, the Type A was made at thirty a day – more than most of his competitors in 1919 and pretty impressive.

Around 23,000 Type As were made before it was replaced by the Type B2 which, with its bored-out 1,452cc engine, could produce a top speed of 44mph, but with the fiscal penalty of a 9CV rating. Continuing the trend Citroën had introduced with the A,

the B2 was available in a variety of body styles and was cheap to run. Due to the advantages of volume production the purchase price was kept low, too. By 1922 the B2 was leaving the production lines at 300 per day.

Wishing to streamline still further the production methods at the Quai de Javel, Citroën investigated more efficient ways of making car bodies. What he had seen of the Budd Company in America had convinced him that all-steel bodywork was far easier and quicker to produce than the steel-clad wooden-framed cars then popular. He signed an agreement with Budd to build all-steel bodies under licence. The new models were known as B10s and were effectively the B2 saloon and open tourer, but with the new steel bodywork. The old B2 and the B10 remained in production until 1925 when both were replaced by a new model, the B12. These featured a lengthened and widened chassis, and shared to some extent the body types of the B2 and B10 ranges. The new model also featured front-wheel brakes.

During the production of the B-models, a simpler, scaled-down model – the C – was released in 1921. This light two-seater was to gain the nickname of *petit citron* (little lemon) – a play on words inspired by the lemon-yellow paintwork in which the majority were finished. Launched with an 856cc side valve engine, the C would appeal to the less well off, and with its light weight and ease of driving it appealed to independent young women, increasing numbers of whom were now driving for themselves. Improvements such as toughened chassis frames and different cabriolet body styles came with the C2 and a longer version known as the C3. An attractive variant of the C3 was the *Trefle* (cloverleaf) with boat-tailed tourer coachwork. More than 80,000 Cs of all types were built by the time production ceased in 1926.

Around this time the B12 was replaced by Jules Salomon's last Citroën design, the B14. At first fitted with an attractive four-door saloon body, the B14 was ultimately offered with more than two dozen different body styles including the B15 20cwt van, the B14F with servo brakes designed by Westinghouse, and the B14G which appeared in 1927 Paris Motor Show with a whole series of revised body styles. The flexibility of being able to offer many body styles was due to Citroën's production methods and the design of the basic unit. The B14 used a two-bearing four-cylinder engine with 70mm bore, giving 1,539cc and a 9CV rating.

1928 saw the arrival of the C4 and C6 models, sporting four-cylinder 10CV and six-cylinder 14CV engines derived from the first Type A units and sharing that model's bore and stroke of 72mm × 100mm to provide 1,628cc and 2,442cc. These models could produce more power due to the sturdy design incorporating additional main bearings to withstand higher crankshaft speeds. Cylinder heads, however, reverted to the previous design of being cast integrally with the block. Short- and long-wheelbase versions were available, and in compliance with accepted Citroën practice they became available over the production run in many different styles and with many improvements. The C6E sported a wider

*1924 Citroën C3 – one of the most popular small Citroëns of the 1920s.*

*1923 C-type 5CV Citroën – the* petit citron *with tiny 856cc side-valve engine. Over 80,000 C-types were built.*

track and body, C4-III received improved instrumentation and the C6F of 1930 had a stronger chassis, an even wider track and body, and other mechanical changes and improved interiors. The C4F followed suit in 1931. The Citroën Grand Luxe incorporated an over-bored engine up to 75mm and was a more luxuriously finished car with better appointments, but still based on the C6F.

*A 1929 C4 model reputed to have covered a million miles.*

These models were all replaced in October 1931 by the C6G to replace the Grand Luxe and the C4G, which received the similarly bored-out engine, but in four-cylinder form. The two had improved front suspension and stronger bodies. A much cheaper basic model was also introduced called the C4-IX, an altogether more simple car.

The six-cylinder car gained a flexible system of engine mountings called Floating Power. This had been designed for Chrysler in America by the Frenchman Lemaire and it returned to France in the C6G when Citroën took out patent rights on the design. The four-cylinder car also benefitted from the system, but the C4-IX base model never had the improvement. Of course, today nearly every engine application has flexible mountings both to isolate engine noise and to absorb vibration and engine movement. In the 1930s the system was new and exciting enough to be called Floating Power!

The C models were a fantastic success even by recent standards. Some 360,000 of both basic types were produced before the C's demise in 1932. This figure owed much to the advanced production methods at Citroën.

## THE ROSALIE

While the C-types were a very great success and helped cement the Citroën name in the world automotive trade, the early 1930s was a time of great innovation and progress in the motor car world, and André Citroën decided that a completely new car should replace the good but just slightly dated Cs.

There were three basic types in the new range, named after their respective horsepower ratings. The least powerful of the three was the 8A which used an engine of the same bore and stroke as the B2, but

*A 1930 12/8 Tourer. A Citroën like this would not have looked out of place on the streets of prohibition Chicago ...*

with improved power up to 32bhp at 3,200rpm. Then came the 10A with the old C4 engine and the 15A with the C6 engine. The cars appeared at the 1932 Paris Motor Show and soon earned the named of 'Rosalie' after the Montlhéry record-breaking car which was based on them. While there were two previous record cars based on the C6 also called Rosalie, the new 'Petit Rosalie' spent 134 days on the track, establishing international long-distance records and covering almost 200,000 miles at an average speed of 57.9mph.

The new Rosalie range once again sported a range of body styles utilizing the latest bodywork technology and constructed to an even sturdier and simpler design than before. Each body used only four major steel panel pressings, and the four-size range started with the smallest for the 8A and 10A, a middle body size for the 10A and the largest two for the 15A.

In comparison with previous Citroën ranges this may seem to be a limited choice, but by clever manipulation of trim levels and by using the approved offerings of outside coachbuilders, the company was able to offer over eighty body styles. Technical improvements were not left behind: torsion bar suspension came to the front of the 8A in 1933 and was added to the 10A two years later. Citroën had also bought patents from the Studebaker company for a freewheel device and fitted it to 15A and larger versions of the 10A. Freewheel enabled the driver to change gear without using the clutch and allowed the car to freewheel down hills, improving fuel consumption and reducing engine wear. The lack of torque in the gearbox enabled the clutchless changes and made the whole persona of the car more relaxed and easier to drive. With no engine braking the driver had to be sure of his brakes, but the system was lockable in or out of freewheel.

*1933 Citroën 'Yacco'. This 8CV, named* Petit Rosalie *and driven by Cesar Marchand on the Montlhéry test track that year, covered 200,000 miles in 134 days at an average of 57.8mph during endurance trials sponsored by the Yacco oil company. Marchand himself wrote on the photograph, 'Thanks to Citroën to make it possible for me to give France the world record. Thanks to Yacco's organization for making it a success.'*

# THE TRACTION AVANT

Citroën's occasional use of unorthodox technology in his car designs was an indication that the company was prepared to stun the motoring world with a new car dramatically different from any that had gone before. The car which next appeared on the scene fitted that bill.

The new project owed its existence to André Citroën's visit to the Budd car company in Detroit. That company had built a prototype to demonstrate its monocoque body construction method allied to innovative front-wheel drive. Impressed, Citroën obtained a licence and assembled a team to see the project through to fruition. He was in a hurry. It would be unheard of today to assemble a team to develop a totally new car in March one year and have it enter production in April of the following year. But it was done between 1933 and 1934. The new car was far from ordinary too: the innovation hinted at by several previous Citroën designs was to come together in this model. It had front-wheel drive, independent torsion bar suspension on all wheels, a steel monocoque structure and a brand-new overhead valve engine. The gearbox had to be of an entirely new type to operate with the front-wheel drive installation.

The team was run by André Lefèbvre, ex-Voisin and Renault, with stylist Flaminio Bertoni, body engineer Raoul Cuinet, engine designer Maurice Sainturat and suspension engineer Maurice Jullien. A fully automatic gearbox was planned for the new model and inventor Robert Dmitri Sensaud de Lavaud provided plans and prototype units. It was, however, dropped at the last minute to be replaced by the three-speed manual unit which made it into production. The monocoque construction itself extended forward into two 'horns', to which the engine and transmission attached for ease of servicing.

The *petit voiture*, as the project was code-named, was developed away from the main factory for secrecy. There were many problems with the first cars but there was a lot of money thrown at the project and they were sorted out in double-quick time. 20,000 units were sold between the press launch in April and the Paris Motor Show in October. The new 7CV Citroën, now generally called the *Traction Avant* for 'front drive', was a huge success.

Rack-and-pinion steering, allied to the front-wheel drive and the new radial tyres which were designed by Michelin for the car made for superb handling and, with the torsion bar suspension, extreme comfort too. The eye-catching body shape was a winner with unrivalled space and, of course, a flat floor inside. The three-speed gearbox operated via a square gate attached to the dashboard. With this lovely to use and very sensible system there is never any question of which gear the car is in. Basically there is a gear in each of the four corners of the gate.

Again, Citroën offered many body styles including longer wheelbase *familiale* models, a hatchback model called the *commerciale*, the *Berline Legére* roadster and the *faux cabriolet* two-seater. The overhead valve four-cylinder 1,911cc engine was unstressed at a low 5.9:1 compression ratio and put out 46bhp. Top speed was just under 80mph. Later models had six-cylinder engines giving prodigious power and performance, but with a thirst to match.

Again, the ever resourceful Citroën, while not being actually involved in the stunt, was happy to help with an amazing publicity exercise to prove the toughness of the new model. Restauranteur Francois Lecot drove his Traction Avant between his restaurant in Lyon and Paris and back one day, and then between there and Monte Carlo and

*The Traction Avant – this is a 1939 7CV – was a revolutionary vehicle of monocoque construction, front-wheel drive and torsion bar suspension. The Traction Avant effectively broke both André Citroën and his company, but was to be a commercial success for the company which bought Citroën, the Michelin tyre company, whose radial ply tyres gave the Traction Avant such good handling.*

back the next day – repeating the itinerary every day. After a year of this relentless schedule – taking time off only to compete in the Monte Carlo Rally, he had driven an amazing 250,000 miles. This incredible marathon was to have been financed by

*The Traction Avant was available in several body styles including this rather superb Berline Legere Roadster. This is a 1938 example.*

André Citroën, Lecot's friend, but Citroën pulled out because of the company's financial problems at the time. The stocky, bereted Lecot did it anyway, mortgaging his restaurant and hotel business to finance the operation. The car he chose was comfortable, easy to drive and could maintain a high average speed even on France's less-than-perfect roads of the time. The Traction was serviced just three times, tyres were changed every 15,000 miles and it didn't falter. The record remains unequalled by any other driver or any other car to this day.

## THE MICHELIN INCIDENT

An ill-advised plan to expand the Quai de Javel works was probably responsible for the downfall of the Société André Citroën. The rebuilding operations were to accommodate the new Traction Avant and also to counter Louis Renault, who had invited Citroën to observe the huge expansion programme at his Billancourt factory. Citroën was to go one better by building enough new factory space to make the new Traction Avant in less than

five months. This, and the astronomical investment poured into the new car project, quite obviously overstretched the pockets of Citroën, who had put a large part of his own fortune into both projects.

Strikes played their own part in the downfall, to say nothing of worsening sales figures and the general depression in Europe during the early 1930s. For Citroën, huge profits of 100 million francs in 1926 had turned into debts of 125 million by 1930. By the end of 1934 a litigious minor creditor had had enough and sued Citroën for his money. This forced the company into liquidation and it was taken over by its major creditor, the Michelin tyre company.

While early cars suffered from the lack of development, prone to breakdowns and mechanical problems, the new Traction Avant eventually proved to be an inherently good design and was a seminal motor car in the history of motorized transport. Citroën disappeared from the scene a broken man, dying, it is said of a broken heart, in 1935. The Traction Avant lived on and made massive profits for its new owners, surviving up to 1956 and being built in Belgium, Germany, Italy and

*Citroën was to continue with front-wheel drive for the incredible DS19 which appeared in 1956. The fabulous new car with a clean, crisp body designed by Bertone sported a 2-litre four-cylinder engine giving 75bhp.*

*Little could be done to improve on the design by the time of this 1967 Pallas model. A few trim strips, hubcaps and rubber overriders were some of the visible changes.*

*The* décapotable *DS Pallas of 1967 was the work of coachbuilder Henri Chapron. Examples are highly sought-after today.*

Poland as well as Slough in England and, of course, Quai de Javel. 700,961 were built in those twenty-two years.

After the take-over by Michelin, the Quai de Javel factories were run jointly by Pierre Michelin and Pierre Boulanger, an ex-Air Force captain, who had joined Edouard Michelin's company in 1919. Having succeeded with Michelin in ensuring that the Traction Avant was the success that such a ground-breaking design deserved to be, Boulanger had the beginnings of a new idea which would come to fruition years later as the 2CV.

## The Citroën-Kegresse Caterpillar Car

The Citroën-Kegresse caterpillar car was an extraordinary vehicle which worked very well and survived in use from its invention in 1922 up to and during World War Two, Germany using it on the Russian front. Designed by the inventive Frenchman Adolphe Kegresse who was in charge of Tsar Nicholas II car collection, it was in response to the Tsar's wish that he could travel by car from Moscow to St Petersburg. The design was simple and consisted of lightweight flexible rubber bands running around sprung bogies driven by the rear axle. The system provided superb off-road ability years before the four-wheel drive vehicle. In Kegresse's own words the cars could 'travel at all speeds either over deep snow and ice or roads covered with lightly packed snow, or on dry and stony roads – and then leave the road and proceed to travel across country without stopping or slowing down.'

The designs were perfected by 1913 and patents were lodged in France and Russia. Events overtook Kegresse, though, and with the Russian Revolution he found himself out of a job, eventually to settle in France. Here he met with Citroën, who was to give him every help with the manufacture of his new idea. Setting up a new company to make the cars, Citroën offered the B2 car as a base for the project and soon the Société Citroën-Kegresse-Hinstin was making the Citroën-Kegresse caterpillar car. A series of demonstrations was held which proved the Kegresse to be an ideal all-terrain vehicle able to travel over sand dunes or snow drifts with ease, and even surmount gradients of more than 45 degrees. The system reduced the power demand in rough conditions and much smaller engines could be used to achieve what, with a traditional form of motive power, would demand much more horsepower. It was for this reason that Citroën chose the tried and tested B2 engine to power the revolutionary Citroën-Kegresse.

The caterpillar car's light weight enabled it not to get bogged down and 'raids' were held across the Alps, the first taking place at Mont Revard in 1921. The successful design was assembled in London, from completely knocked-down kits supplied from France, by the British subsidiary Citroën-Kegresse Ltd. Customers included the Royal Artillery and other sectors of the British Army.

An even more ambitious test was achieved in 1923 when a team of caterpillar cars led by Citroën's Director General of the gear making and car assembly factories, Georges-Marie Haardt, set out to prove that a motorized trans-Sahara expedition was possible. Starting and finishing at Touggourt, south of Algiers, the team gained Timbuktu in twenty days and, by the time it returned to Touggourt, had travelled 4,300 miles in forty days.

*This ex-French Army 1926 Citroën-Kegresse was used as a shooting brake by the Duke of Buccleuch, for timber hauling and for snow rescue work. Seated in the back are the Duke and Master Nicholas Phipps.*

# 2   Evolution of the 2CV

## BOULANGER'S IDEA

The conception of the 2CV took place against the backdrop of a large, principally rural country. France will always be more rural than the small island of Britain. It has much more space, and in the mid-1930s those spaces felt even greater than they do now. Country people used bicycles or the horse and cart to transport themselves and their goods from place to place. Very few owned cars, and the ones that did exist had to cope with unmetalled roads and years of neglect.

When Citroën Managing Director Pierre Boulanger visited his local market town and watched the farmers and smallholders bringing their goods to town in handcarts or by horse and cart he reasoned that a very cheap, very tough and very simple car would sell fantastically well. But could Citroën

*The Citroën factory on the Seine at Quai de Javel. River and railway met the road here and a barge is moored, perhaps unloading. Parked in the road under the Citroën sign are half a dozen four-light 2CVs and a Fourgonnette – and a rogue Renault 4CV, dating the picture to the very early 1950s. To the right of the main white building and almost lost amongst the factory buildings nestles an attractive mansard-roofed town house with curved bay windows.*

make it? The idea of a car designed for the majority of France's population – farmers and country folk – had a spark of life.

He talked it over with his Chief Engineer, Maurice Broglie. Boulanger's request was a pretty tall order when you consider the sort of cars that were being built by Citroën at the time. He decided to make a series of specifications which would be important to the people who he imagined would be buying the car. The now well-known set of instructions comprised the following: the car should be able to carry two peasants, 50kg of potatoes and a box of eggs; with this load it should be able to be driven at 60kph and return a fuel consumption of 3ltr × 100km (over 90mpg!); and it had to do all this over the worst roads rural France had to offer. He further specified that if the car were driven over a ploughed field, not a single egg in the box would be broken. The car should be simple to drive for both the farmer and his wife, and also simple to maintain. The appearance was not important but, of course, cheapness was. Boulanger said that what he wanted was 'four wheels under an umbrella'. What he eventually got was nearly everything he had specified.

As early as the 1920s André Citroën had ideas for such unheard-of things as an organized network of dealers and an organized repair manual and parts catalogue. He was doing these things in his methodical way long before other manufacturers even thought of them. He also organized market surveys – today part and parcel of the launch of a new product. He had a market survey department and its head, Jacques Duclos, was asked to organize an extensive survey throughout France. He asked different sorts of people everywhere what they wanted from a small car. Some 10,000 were interviewed, and questions asked about their preferences and wants from a motor car.

# DEVELOPMENT STARTS

While Duclos was busy with the survey – and it took him five months to do – the design team began work in strict secrecy. Boulanger gathered around him the best team he could. At its head was André Lefèbvre, who took responsibility from Maurice Broglie. Boulanger believed in *un homme vehicule*, a figure in overall charge of the whole project, so as there was *un homme Traction Avant* there also came into being *un homme Deux Chevaux* in the shape of Marcel Chinon, a former engineer of the Amilcar company. He was later to contribute much to the design of the vehicle including the final type of unique fore-and-aft linked suspension and he was commonly known as the father of the 2CV, while Boulanger was perhaps its godfather! Under Chinon was Jean Muratet, the bodywork engineer, and the Italian stylist, Flaminio Bertoni, later to be the designer of the seminal DS/ID Citroëns of the late 1950s and 1960s. Alphonse Forceau was a gear specialist and Roger Prud'homme, the head of the experimental workshop. The project became known as the TPV for *toute petite voiture* ('very small car').

Designs were drawn up for a front wheel drive car – mimicking the Traction Avant – of semi-chassisless construction and weighing in at 300kg. There was no rear axle and extensive use was made of corrugated aluminium to give the body strength. The use of aluminium was important from the weight-saving point of view, but it was nearly always expensive to buy and particularly difficult to weld. A wooden mock-up was built at the workshops in the Rue du Théatre, and it was not until 1937 that a working prototype was built, some time before there was an engine to power it. The prototype had magnesium axle arms, seats strung hammock-like from

*2CV Citroën and the 1949 Wimille prototypes at the Malartre museum.*

the roof and mica windows instead of glass. A torsion-bar suspension had been devised by Alphonse Forceau and took up space under the rear seat.

Fitted with a 500cc BMW motorcycle engine as a test hack, the car was capable of over 60mph – fairly frightening for a vehicle with only front wheel brakes and simplistic steering, but not surprising given its light fabric body stretched over an alloy framework. Engine designs for the TPV settled on a twin-cylinder water-cooled unit designed by Maurice Sainturat – who had designed the Traction Avant engine – after ideas for a single-cylinder engine had been shelved. This new engine went into the twenty or so prototypes built by the end of 1937; these were now looking like proper cars, now clad in aluminium bodywork.

As secrecy was getting harder to preserve with the new project, testing was done in the grounds of a chateau, long since demolished, outside Paris and to the west, at Ferté-Vidame. Testing began in March 1938 with the very basic machines making life for the testers very cold and miserable. Problems soon appeared with the suspension, and adjusting the torsion bar arrangement

front and rear never cured it. A curious hydraulic anti-dive device also failed to make any improvement. The welded aluminium chassis platform was not good at withstanding the twisting and flexing of continued testing, and splits appeared along the weld seams. Various strengthening additions were helping, but also increasing the weight at each step.

Apparently Boulanger was happy with progress and a launch date of late 1939 was envisaged with production in the early spring. A test run of 250 cars was ordered by Boulanger and construction began on these at the Levallois plant. More problems became obvious when the bodies began to be made. Aluminium is notoriously difficult to spot weld and the workers found themselves having to construct many panels by hand, as the jigs were not yet made.

Pre-production models had the 375cc water-cooled engine with a lawnmower-type cord starter, later discarded because ladies complained of broken fingernails – so the story goes! A starter handle replaced it. Rack-and-pinion steering and torsion bar suspension mounted on the duralinox platform chassis was retained, while hydraulic front and lever-operated rear brakes were fitted. The body was of alloy but the wings were in steel. The entire roof was of canvas from the top of the windscreen to the rear bumper rail. The French traffic laws not requiring more, only one headlight was fitted, being matched by a single hand-operated windscreen wiper. Door handles and locks were also missing: to open the door the hinged mica window panel had first to be raised.

## THE WAR INTERVENES

Many have said that the outbreak of war prevented Citroën making a fool of itself with the TPV. There were too many problems with it and there was too much haste in getting it into production. Production and design needed many more months work to perfect, and in the end just one of the 250 TPVs ordered was completed when, at 11 o'clock in the morning on 3 September 1939, Britain and France declared war on Germany. The next few months were confusing for the TPV project. After the invasion of France, Boulanger ordered the destruction of the 249 uncompleted pilot cars. Three, however, survived – one at the factory,

where it was used as a tyre-testing hack by Michelin and disguised against prying German eyes with a crude bonnet. Two others were found after the war in the Clermont-Ferrand region. The Michelin tyre-testing prototype was bought in 1946 by the Musée Henri Malartre at Rochetailée, near Lyons.

Citroën had withdrawn from Paris to Niort, and under the Occupation was unable to proceed with car production, under orders from the Vichy government. Boulanger was a staunch supporter of de Gaulle and was determined not to let the TPV fall into German hands; despite his best efforts, it is likely at least one was seen by the Germans. They are unlikely to have thought much of it, however. The Germans took away the big body-tooling presses which had been used for the Traction Avant and despatched them to Germany. Some time during the night before departure in the Paris marshalling yards, the labels on the wagons were changed with the result that the different components of the press tools were despatched to far flung corners of the German countryside, and even outside Germany. It is said that Boulanger was responsible for this covert operation. It is also said that when Citroën factories were

*The single-headlamp prototype. Fitted with the Sainturat-designed water-cooled engine this car, ordered destroyed by Pierre Boulanger, survived and was rebuilt in 1948 on the orders of Citroën's Publicity Chief Jacques Wolgensinger. It was rediscovered in the 1970s and its engine and ancillaries were found in boxes in a storeroom. Citroën uses the car for publicity.*

*The 1936 pick-up prototype with water-cooled engine. At this stage prototypes were definitely lash-ups.*

put over to building 3- and 4-ton trucks, the production lines were plagued with difficulties and proceeded incredibly slowly, and the completed trucks were badly put together, resulting in frequent breakdowns.

The Vichy government had forbidden the design or manufacture of new vehicles but the redoubtable Boulanger did not let that stop him from resuming development on the TPV. Testing was secretly carried out in the Auvergne mountains near the Michelin factories. Boulanger, like many at the beginning of the war, thought that it would not last long, but by 1941 it was clear that France was in for a long ordeal at the hands of the Third Reich. Covertly, Boulanger made a few steps toward continuing with the development of the TPV. One of the first was to discover if the build costs as originally envisaged had remained the same after the few years of development. To his dismay it was discovered that the TPV was now going to cost some 40 per cent more than its original specification. It was clear that the aluminium platform chassis and body panels were, due to the cost and complexity of working with the material, the prime reason why costs had risen so drastically. While

Boulanger and Lefèbvre tried to defend the aluminium version with its magnesium alloy suspension arms as not only lightweight but rust-resistant too, that avenue of construction was dismissed and an all-steel version was drawn up by Maurice Steck, new head of the bodywork section.

Obviously most of these changes only occurred on paper as actual development was very difficult under the circumstances. Many other possibilities were explored during the war while Boulanger was doing his Gaullist best to quietly sabotage and slow up production at the truck factories.

A major discovery during the pre-war winter testing of the water-cooled engines had been that they were near impossible to start when the temperature was below 5°C. Now at Citroën, Walter Becchia used his considerable intuitive skill to put an air-cooled flat-twin engine design together within days. Having the same 375cc capacity as the water-cooled unit, Becchia's design was of such simple and rugged construction that its success was practically guaranteed. Development of the water-cooled design was halted; though nothing further was done with it, a few did survive in the remaining pre-war prototypes.

Another area of considerable change was in the gearbox. Becchia knew that his new design would need a four-speed gearbox and set about redesigning that, too. Of course Boulanger was very opposed to it, saying that all previous Citroëns had made do with three speeds and that a fourth was unnecessary and would needlessly complicate the specification. But Becchia knew of Boulanger's predictable reaction and told him that it was in fact a three-speed gearbox with *surmultipliée* – overdrive. And he really wasn't lying to his boss either: when the car was put into production after the war the fourth *surmultipliée* gear didn't improve the top speed noticably, but engine revolutions were considerably lower. The first production models had an 'S' on the gear knob in place of a '4'.

The third major area for work was the suspension. Problems had been experienced with the torsion bar springing and the rates could not be accurately set. Its characteristics also changed a lot when the car was fully laden. Later, a system of compression springs was tried to a design by Alphonse Forceau. These were linked front and rear, and although the system was much cheaper to put into production than the torsion bar set-up, the roadholding was just not right. Léon Renault was put on the job of improving the suspension, and he proposed a system of enclosed spring dampers for each wheel, but linked front and rear. War broke out, however, and the system never made it into a prototype. Renault was called for national service and did not return to

*Ken Smith, who knew all the occupants, provided the description for this photograph: 'At the wheel is Marcel Chinon. He was co-ordinator of the 2CV programme. He had contributed much to the design of the vehicle, including the final type of unique fore-and-aft linked suspension. Next to him is Madame Gaulon, secretary to Boulanger and later to M.M.P. Bercot and A. Brueder, his successors. In the back nearest the camera is Jean Cadiou, head of the* Bureau d' Etudes. *Beside him is Jacques Duclos who was head of the Market Survey Department and who had carried out, on behalf of Michelin, the very first customer survey in the Thirties'.*

Citroën until 1945, when he found his ideas had been all but forgotten and that the TPV was still experiencing difficulties in the area of suspension. Again he put his ideas to Boulanger; they were approved and the unique system was in place in prototypes by 1947. It made it into production and remained almost unaltered until 1975.

## POST-WAR PROGRESS

Development continued apace after the war, and although the press tools which had been scattered through Europe by Boulanger's efforts after the occupation did eventually return to Paris, they were needed for the production lines of the Traction Avant, which had many curved panels. So the 2CV remained with its basically slab-sided body and consequently utilized a minimum of press tooling.

The single headlamp was replaced by twin lamps as testers noted that oncoming traffic at night reacted as if there was a motorcycle coming towards them. One tester with cold feet had rigged up a tube running from the exhaust manifold to the interior of the cabin to warm his feet, and the basic idea was retained for the production cars. The TPV was eventually approved by Pierre Boulanger and the new car was to be unveiled at the Paris Motor Show of 1948. Boulanger called it simply the *Deux Chevaux*.

At least one of the show cars had a lawn-mower-type cord starter operated from inside the car, while the favoured method of starting the engine was still the handle at the front. Boulanger realized that both methods were archaic, even for the 2CV, and he demanded an ordinary electric starter. Becchia had designed the engine to make such a fitment possible.

### Walter Becchia

The brilliant and innovative engine designer, Walter Becchia, had come to Citroën from Talbot in 1941. His history with Talbot is worth recalling. After the collapse of Sunbeam Talbot Darracq Antonio Lago – who had a profitable business in London importing Talbots and Darracqs – managed to persuade the board to allow him to run the factory at Suresnes on the outskirts of Paris. The first car bearing the Talbot-Lago name was modelled heavily on the SS1 – produced by the company later to become Jaguar. But the way ahead in Lago's view was through racing and the pedigree it would establish. In 1934 Becchia, as Chief Engine Designer, was put to designing an engine which would give the Mercedes-Benz and Auto Union racing teams a run for their money. He used a Fiat 23CV block and added his patented OHV top end using cross-pushrods. The result was a 4-litre, 160bhp motor that cried out to be raced. Lago persuaded Réné Dreyfus to leave Scuderia Ferrari and be Talbot's number one driver. The next few years brought many victories

with the new engine, culminating in a 1-2-3 success in the 1938 Comminges Grand Prix at St Gaudens, with Louis Chiron heading the list. That engine in similar form remained in production right into the 1950s in the Talbot Lago Grand Sport, one of the last grand routier motor cars with such a long pedigree.

Becchia's work at Talbot-Lago must have been appreciated, but the company at the time was leading an extremely fragile financial existence. Lago must have been a brilliant entrepreneur to keep the company on its feet and to keep the suppliers delivering, probably without payment, for months. As life there was very much hand-to-mouth with every moment taken one day at a time, it is to be imagined that when Antonio Lago asked for something to be done it was done very quickly with as much available skill as could be mustered. It was not the sort of company that could spend months or years in research. It is perhaps this trial by fire which made Becchia's work so quickly and so perfectly done.

# 3   The Car Described

To understand the simple and rugged Becchia design that was to power the car that mobilized rural France, we can go back to the most detailed description of the engine in existence, that of the *Automobile Engineer* in 1954 which by the looks of it dismantled a complete 2CV to see what made it tick:

> One of the most important areas to consider in the front-wheel drive layout is the flexible mounting of the engine. The rear of the 2CV engine compartment is a busy area where the components for the rack-and-pinion steering, the crosstube of the suspension pivot, the gearbox and other ancillaries vie for space on the bulkhead. Here, the rear mounting is fitted, carried by a swan-neck fitting welded on top of the crosstube supporting the front suspension pivots. The end of this fitting projects into the rear of the central steel tube of the mounting bush, where it is secured by two 7mm-diameter set bolts passed from the front through a vertical plate welded in the tube. When the engine is installed, it is lowered so that two bolts, screwed into the rear face of the turret housing for the striker lever of the gear shift control, rest in U-shaped slots cut in the top edge of a vertical plate welded to the steel outer tube of the rear mounting bush. The bolts are then tightened against the plate.
>
> The front mountings not only have to control the axial movement of the engine as it moves in response to different throttle openings and load bearings, but they have to react to the torque movement of the front-wheel drive layout. To effect this a V-arrangement has been adopted with double-sandwich rubber mountings each side. The centre plate and the rubber above and below it are enclosed in a short, rectangular

*Photo from above showing the whole car opened up – an early fabric-booted French 2CV.*

*A pre-December 1960 AZL,*
*before the new fluted bonnet.*

section tubular housing which is bolted to a bracket on the front cross-member of the frame. On each side, the centre plate is bent upwards and flanged outwards. A stud is welded to the top face of each flange, and these studs are used to secure the unit to a right-angle bracket bolted to the front wall of the crankcase. The upturned ends of the centre plate act as limit stops to prevent the amplitude of oscillation of the engine about its longitudinal axis becoming very large. The reaction at the front to the final drive torque is taken by rubber in compression either above or below the centre plate, according to the direction of the drive.

Becchia's genius in using one unit to do more than one task is illustrated by the dynamo's having no bearings of its own, being an extension of the crankshaft:

An integral crankcase and sump is of cast aluminium alloy divided vertically in the longitudinal plane, the two halves being dowelled together. At the rear, four 10mm studs are carried to secure the transmission casing to the crankcase. The two housings are cored in the front end of the crankcase. The inner one, the base of which is open to the sump, completely encloses the driving gear on the crankcase extension and the half-speed wheel. Behind the driving gear is the front bearing of the crankshaft, and in front of this is a ring pressed on to the shaft. This ring has an oil return scroll machined on its periphery; it is housed in a bore in the front wall of the crankcase.

In front of this is the dynamo, the hub of which is on a taper on the end of the crankshaft. A forward extension of the hub carries the blower rotor, and is internally tapered to receive a tapered plug pulled into it by a bolt screwed into the front end of the crankshaft. Dogs for the starter handle are formed on the plug. The shell of the dynamo, in which the field coils are mounted, is bolted to the crankcase. With this arrangement there are no bearings in the dynamo and therefore reliability may be improved and cost reduced.

The crankshaft and connecting rods, together with the front journal bearing and the pressed-on helical gear and oil return scroll ring at the front, are fitted to the engine as a complete assembly and the components cannot be ordered separately as spares. This is because the crankshaft is made up from five pieces, and the connecting rods and big-end bearing bushes are assembled on to the crank pins before they are pressed into the webs. The five pieces are the front and rear ends, complete with webs, the two crank pins and the oval centre web. In an engine of much higher output the press fit alone would be unable to resist the torque loading of the shaft, but in this application the components do not move relative to one another. [In other words the engineers didn't really know why it didn't twist – it just didn't!]

The axes of the main journal bearings are in the plane on which the crankcase is divided. Axial location of the shaft is effected by the front bearing, which is flanged at each end. Both bearings are of white-metal-lined bronze and are located by shouldered dowels. The larger portion of each dowel is in the bearing housing while the smaller portion is in the bearing, so there is no possibility of the dowel contacting the journal and scoring it. By using white-metal-lined bearings, a certain amount of misalignment of the shaft can be tolerated and in the 2CV they are large enough to cater for considerable out-of-balance forces.

Both the front and rear ends of the crankshaft are counterbored to reduce weight. At the rear, an oil thrower ring is pressed on and is located against a shoulder immediately behind the rear journal. This thrower works in a space cored in the crankcase. Immediately behind it is a lip-type oil seal, which is housed in the crankcase, and which bears on the tail end of the shaft. The flywheel is spigoted on to the end of the shaft, and secured by five 8mm set bolts and located by one 8mm dowel. The five bolts are locked by a circular plate, the edges of which are turned up against the flats of the bolt heads. The ring gear has 107 teeth, is pressed on and meshes with a nine-toothed pinion.

The big end bearing housings are not split, but are of the ring type. With this

*The 1959 dashboard, one of the simplest possible groups of controls. The speedometer at top left also drove the windscreen wipers, or they could be operated by hand. The single-stalk, column-mounted light and horn control pre-dated by decades the control used on most cars today.*

arrangement, the bearing lengths can be kept to a minimum because there is no discontinuity in the housing, and also because no bolts have to be accommodated. A further reduction in length has been obtained by the use of copper load-bearing shells. As a result the offset of the cylinder axes, and therefore of the rocking couples, is relatively small. Phosphor bronze bushes are fitted in the small ends of the I-section connecting rods. Fully floating gudgeon pins are retained by wire circlips in grooves in the piston bosses.

Aluminium alloy pistons with domed crowns are used. They are unusual in that at the thrust faces, the base of the skirt of each piston is extended downwards. This is presumably to increase the bearing area available to take the thrust, or it could be to improve piston cooling, but the greater proportion of heat flow to the cylinder walls takes place through the rings and not between the contacting faces of the piston and bore.

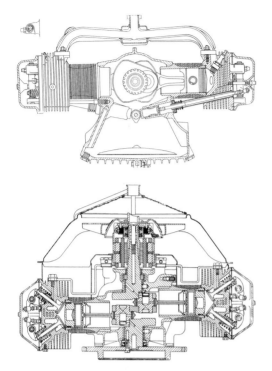

*Arrangement of the 2CV engine, from the March 1954* Automobile Engineer.

The contact breaker cam and automatic advance and retard mechanism are mounted on a forward extension of the camshaft. Behind these is machined an oil return scroll that works in a bore in the front wall of the crankcase. Immediately to the rear of this is the eccentric on which bears the push rod that actuates the fuel pump mounted on a boss on the right-hand side of the crankcase above the crankshaft gear.

The front journal is of such a diameter that the half speed wheel, which is pressed on to it, may be passed over the eccentric during assembly. A noteworthy feature of this half speed wheel is that it is in effect two wheels placed together on a common boss. These wheels are free to rotate independently before assembly to the engine,

and after assembly they can still rotate relative to one another within the limits imposed by the meshing of the teeth. They are sprung in such a way that the trailing flanks of the meshing teeth of one wheel are loaded against the leading flanks of those on the driven wheel, and the leading flanks on the other part of the half speed wheel are loaded against the trailing flanks of the driving wheel. Thus there is no backlash and the timing gear runs silently. The springs are of the coil type and are in tension. There are three of them housed in tangential slots in the wheel discs; one end of each is hooked into a hole in one disc and the other end is similarly attached to the other disc.

At the front of the camshaft, a bush-type bearing is employed. It is located between the half speed wheel and a flange on the rear end of the journal. Axial location of the whole assembly is effected by a stepped dowel, the small diameter portion of which registers in a hole in the bearing, and the larger end is in the housing. The rear end of the camshaft bears directly in the oil pump body, and the eccentric gear of the pump is keyed on to a rearward extension of the shaft.

The tappets are of unusual design of tubular construction and have hardened pads in their ends. Hardened spherical ends are carried at both ends of the push rods. They are housed in tubes, shouldered at each end. The outer end of each tube is pressed and spigoted into the cylinder head, and affixed by peening. Over the inner end is passed a washer, which is located against a shoulder on the tube and retains a coil spring. The inner end of this spring bears on an assembly comprising a sealing ring and cupped retainer washer, round the end of the tube, and presses it against the end face of the tappet housing bored in the crankcase.

The outer end of each push rod sits in the cupped end of a tappet adjusting screw on one end of the rocker arm. This arm is centrally pivoted and on its other end a cone is formed with its apex pointing inwards towards the head. The cone sits in a hole in a retainer washer for a light, coil return spring, which has the function of ensuring that the rocker at all times remains seated on the end of the push rod. On the other end of the boss of the rocker is another arm, extended in the same direction as the one with the cone end; it has a hardened end pad that bears on the valve in the usual way.

There are two rocker shafts per cylinder. They are 12mm in diameter by 100mm long. Their axes are vertical and they are carried between the two valves, which are set at an included angle of 70 degrees in a horizontal plane. The pedestals that support the rocker shafts are cast integrally with the aluminium alloy head, and the upper pair form bosses through which two of the three cylinder holding-down studs are passed. Accessibility to the studs is therefore good.

During assembly, each rocker shaft is inserted from below. When the end of the shaft has been pushed a short distance through the hole in the lower pedestal, a compression coil spring, with a thrust washer at its lower end, is placed over it. Then the rocker, with another washer on its upper end, is inserted between the upper pedestal and the spring, and the shaft is pressed through until its upper end projects a short distance above the pedestal. Thus the rocker and shaft oscillate together. The upper end of each shaft is stepped, so its cross-section is of semi-circular form to clear the cylinder head stud. A hole is drilled radially through it, and the inner end of a spiral spring is inserted in the hole. The outer end of this spring is bent at right angles to the plane of the spiral and is turned behind the rocker pedestal. On earlier models, a split pin was used in this hole to prevent the shaft and rocker assembly from bouncing downwards on the spring when the vehicle traversed rough terrain. Presumably the change was made because of a tendency under certain conditions for the pin to chafe against the

*The 2CV was available with its own-design radio – the* Radioën *– but it took up a lot of space!*

*Early 2CV details: the rear lamp, surrounded by the tubular bumper.*

Three cylinder studs are employed and they are waisted to 8mm between the ends. They pass through the cylinder heads and are screwed into the crankcase. To prevent seepage of oil down the studs, cap nuts are used to hold down the cylinder head and barrel assembly. A single 7mm-diameter stud is screwed into the centre of the cylinder head and a cap nut on it holds down the rocker cover. A joint washer is fitted between the head and cover to prevent loss of oil. If this washer is not in good condition it would be theoretically possible to lose all the lubricating oil from the engine.

A spherical combustion chamber is incorporated in the head, and it was necessary to machine a small recess in the crown of the piston to provide clearance for the upper edge of each valve during the overlap period at top dead centre. The head is spigoted on to the cast iron cylinder barrel, and a 1mm-thick copper gasket is fitted. This, together with the thickening of the barrel section adjacent to the cylinder head joint, ensures that there is an adequate path for the flow of heat from the head into the barrel, where it is dispersed by the cooling fins. Dissipation of heat from the cylinder head is, of course, a major problem in either water- or air-cooled engines.

In the cylinder head, the ports are turned upwards from the valve seats. The exhaust ports discharge vertically at the front and the inlets at the rear. A single joint washer bridges the two joint faces machined on the upper surface of the head, and the inlet and exhaust manifolds are pulled down on to it by three nuts and 7mm-diameter studs. One of these studs is screwed into the joint face in front of the exhaust port, another is screwed into the face behind the inlet port and the third is between the two, where the joint flanges abut.

Both the inlet and exhaust manifolds are fabricated from steel tube and sheet

rocker pedestal. The larger area of contact between the spiral and the pedestal should be sufficient to prevent serious chafing.

Single springs are employed on the valves. In the exhaust valve assembly, the lower end of the spring bears on a shroud which fits over the end of the valve guide to prevent it from being over-oiled, but in the inlet assembly the spring sits on a plain washer round the end of the guide. Each spring is retained by a shouldered washer, in which a hole is drilled eccentrically. A slot is cut in the centre of the washer to break out into the hole, and two flats are machined near the end of the valve stem. After the stem has been passed into the eccentric hole, it slides into the slot in which it is retained by the end of the stem dropping into a counterbore in the centre of the washer.

metal. The inlet pipes from each side pass over the engine and are welded to the riser pipe at the centre. This junction is enclosed in a heater jacket, also fabricated from sheet steel, through which is passed the exhaust gas from the right hand cylinder. On earlier models, a metal screen was interposed between this jacket and the carburettor mounted above it, but it is no longer provided, since it has been found unnecessary. The Solex carburettor is held down by two 7mm diameter studs; a 6mm-thick insulating washer is interposed between it and the riser pipe. A simple felt element-type air cleaner is fitted on top of the carburettor.

A shouldered rubber sleeve connects a pipe from the air silencer to a branch pipe on the oil filler tube assembly bolted on top of the crankcase. In the end of the branch pipe is a simple disc-type non-return valve to ensure that air can only pass out of the crankcase. This is an important feature because there is no oil filter in the lubrication system. [Later models had an external cartridge-type filter.]

An interesting feature of the induction system is a small pipe that carries hot air, to prevent icing in extremely cold weather, to a point immediately above the entrance to the air tube in the centre of the diffuser. This pipe is clipped to the underside of the air cleaner. One end is extended horizontally through a hole in the side of the down pipe and bent at right angles over the diffuser. The other end is also bent downwards at right angles and is connected by a rubber sleeve to a vertical pipe welded to a small jacket clipped on to the exhaust pipe on the right-hand side. This jacket is a small pressing of semi-cylindrical form. One end, and the straight edges which are parallel to the axis of the pipe, are lipped inwards. The other end is left open so that hot air can be drawn into it over the hot exhaust pipe and then up the vertical tube into the carburettor intake.

An extremely simple control linkage connects the organ-type throttle pedal to the lever on the stem of the butterfly valve of the carburettor. It consists of a single rod with one end bent at right angles and inserted into a rubber bush, carried in an eye formed at the upper end of the pressed steel pedal. It is retained by a split pin and washer on the end of the rod. Screwed onto the other end is a ball socket by which it is attached to the lever on the carburettor.

Exhaust gas from the right-hand cylinder is carried through a pipe, over the top of the engine to the heater box, which is round the junction between the induction pipes and the riser. It then passes out through another pipe to the left-hand side, where it is joined by a branch from the other cylinder. The manifold pipe terminates a short distance in front of this junction. A spherical seating ring is welded on its end, and the belled end of the exhaust pipe is clamped to it by means of a diametrically split ring of channel section. Two bolts hold together the halves of the ring. The exhaust pipe is carried forwards and then downwards to the rear, to an expansion box under the left-hand cylinder. From this box, another pipe carries the exhaust into the silencer which is mounted transversely beneath the gearbox.

*Early door handle.*

Lubricating engine oil is drawn through a strainer in the base of the sump into a long, thimble fitting on which the strainer is mounted and thence through a radial hole in the fitting into a vertical passage drilled in the rear wall of the sump and crankcase casting. From this passage, it passes into the eccentric-gear-type oil pump. The gear is keyed on to the rear end of the camshaft. It drives an internally toothed annulus which is free to rotate in the housing, and which meshes at the top of the gear. Below, a crescent-section separator vane fills the clearance between the tips of the teeth of the gear and the annulus.

The oil outlet channel is cored in the cover plate and directs the lubricant into the hollow camshaft. Radial holes in the front end of the camshaft pass the oil into a large-section annular groove round its front journal. From this groove, the lubricant passes into a drilled passage in the end of which is a spring-loaded ball-type relief valve housed in the side of the crankcase. Adjustment of the valve is effected by interposing different distance washers between the end of the spring and the cap nut in which it is housed.

From this valve the oil passes forwards to the banjo connection on the right-hand side of the front wall of the crankcase, and thence to the oil cooler mounted above the crankshaft, between the blower and the crankcase. The outlet from the oil cooler passes to a banjo connection on the left side of the engine where passages are drilled to the main bearing journals. Holes in the crankshaft carry the oil to the hollow crank pins, and radial drillings distribute it outwards to the big end bearings.

Small pipe-connections taken from each of the banjo unions serving the cooler distribute oil through small-diameter pipes to the cylinder head. From the union in each head, drillings take the lubricant to an annular groove round the exhaust valve guide, whence it is passed through holes into the rocker chamber. The oil return to the sump is through the tubes that enclose the push rods. Air is distributed from the eight-bladed, pressed steel rotor to the oil cooler and to the cylinders through a pressed steel shroud ring. A wire mesh stone guard is fitted over the air intake, and in its centre, supported by three stays, is a guide tube for the starter handle.

## THAT UNIQUE SUSPENSION

Although the suspension units evolved over the years, the basic principle is the same and here the way that early suspension units operate is detailed; later ones differ only in detail fittings. In particular, the volute springs were replaced in the later models by rubber blocks which did the same job with perhaps longer life and certainly without any corrosion problems.

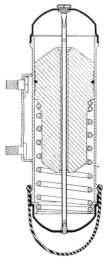

*The dynamic absorber fitted to each wheel counters the smaller movements of the wheel in motion.*

The design of the 2CV suspension is nothing if not inventive. Arranged with the need to reduce unsprung weight to a minimum, the system comprises inboard drum brakes at the front with wheels attached to curved arms connecting to suspension swivels located across the chassis. The pivots of these units incorporate friction dampers. At each wheel is a drum-like cylinder which contains a cast iron weight of 7.75lb, which rests on a coil spring. As the wheel rises, the weight descends in the cylinder and compresses the coil spring against the bottom of the cylinder thus resisting wheel movement. Then as the wheel returns, the mass moves up and places the spring in tension. In other words, the movement of the mass weight is always in anti-phase to that of the suspension and the load in the spring therefore opposes the wheel hop motion. Cleverly, a small quantity of oil is maintained in the cylinder which is forced up the hollow central support tube by the descending weight and sprayed out on to the cylinder walls to act as a lubricant.

These dampers are only designed to suppress wheel patter – as on cobbled roads – that can arise with such a light suspension assembly. The friction dampers within the suspension swivels deal with greater wheel movement. Where the curved suspension arm meets the swivel, a rod is connected from a point on the lower side of the unit, to the main suspension springs – one each side – arranged within cylinders fitted fore and aft beside the chassis rail midway along the car. Inside, two coil springs are attached to front and rear suspension rods. Front and rear suspension is thus linked by the central spring retainer. As a front wheel strikes a bump, the suspension arm rises and compresses the foremost spring. This does two things: it draws the cylinder casing forward against the pressure of a volute spring between the cylinder and the two chassis

outriggers in which the units sit. This in turn compresses the spring attached to the rear wheel, bracing it against the shock of the bump as the car moves forward.

Therefore, as the car goes over the proverbial ploughed field the rear wheels are loaded with more springing power to counteract any tendency to pitch fore and aft. In the absence of a ploughed field a fine demonstration can be carried out in the early 2CV by driving at about 30–35mph over one of those sharp but narrow 'sleeping policemen' (as distinct from modern speed humps, over which driving at such speeds could have rather different results!). You can hear the thump of both wheels as the ridge is traversed but that is all – the car itself keeps an even keel and is unaffected.

*Automobile Engineer* continues:

## BODYWORK

The design of the body is noteworthy for a number of original features and for the ingenuity displayed in solving the design problems, many of which are peculiar to this vehicle. Both the headlamps, for instance, are mounted on a horizontal tube which can be rotated by means of a control rod to adjust the angle of elevation of the beam from inside the car. This is necessary because the suspension layout is such that the attitude of the vehicle varies appreciably with the load.

A radiator muff is included in the toolkit. The battery carrier is tinned and the bonnet treated with anti-corrosive paint in the areas adjacent to the battery. There are towing eyes at front and rear of the chassis, and the spare wheel is housed between the frame side members so that the luggage capacity in the boot is as large as possible and the floor relatively flat. However, it is necessary to unload the luggage to remove the wheel.

Felt-covered ducts carry warm air from behind the engine cylinders to the dash. Among the other amenities provided in the body is a ventilator extending the whole width of the vertical portion of the scuttle immediately below the windscreen. This ventilator may be opened or closed at will and is fitted with a gauze to prevent flies from entering the body. A cabriolet-type hood is fitted. It may be rolled back to uncover only the front portion of the roof, or it can rolled back further to a position immediately above the rear light. An extension of this cover is used to serve as a bootlid. The lower half of the window on each of the front doors is hinged horizontally; a rubber clip at the top of the door can be used to hold the window in the open position. In general, the body panels are of simple form so that wear of the press tools is reduced to a minimum. Moreover, since most of the panels are relatively flat, repair to damage done during service should be easy.

The seats are exceptionally comfortable for this class of car. They might be described as a cross between the bench and bucket types. The two front seats are formed by a single tubular structure based on three vertical longitudinal frames, one on each side and another midway between them. These three support the seat and squab frames, which carry rubber strips, in

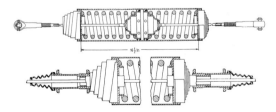

*The unique 2CV suspension 'pots'. This early type has the external volute springs which were replaced by rubber versions in later cars.*

tension, with a canvas overlay. The rubber deflects to conform to the shape of the body and thereby gives a degree of support similar to that afforded by a bucket seat. Because of the extreme softness of this arrangement, the passengers are well insulated from engine vibration and road shocks too severe to be adequately dealt with by the engine mountings and suspension system. A peg, welded under the lower horizontal member of each side frame of the seat, is bent forwards at right angles and registers in one of five holes punched in a row in the side frame of the chassis. These five holes are provided for adjustment of the seat position. The rear seats are similar to the front ones except that they are mounted on a raised platform and the lower ends of the three frames form legs instead of being joined by horizontal members. These ends register in holes in the platform, and the seat is secured by a quick-release catch on the rear leg of the centre frame. Collars are welded round the legs to act as stops to limit the depth of the legs in the holes.

**TRANSMISSION**

The clutch is unusual in that instead of being housed in a dished pressed-steel casing, it is in the cupped flywheel, the rear of which is closed by a steel plate secured by ten 6mm-diameter set bolts. A fairly conventional centre plate, faced on each side with a 160mm-diameter friction lining, is employed. The centre of the plate is dished to the rear and riveted to a splined hub carried on a shaft overhung from the final drive unit.

Six pressure springs are employed. They are housed in flanged thimbles in holes in the rear cover, and bear against the pressure plate. The rear cover and pressure plate assembly is held together by three special bolts with round heads countersunk

*Later-type window catch, more complicated with a spring and catch.*

in the front face of the plate, and the threaded ends of the bolts are passed through holes in the ends of the three withdrawal levers. A coil spring is fitted round the shank of each bolt between the rear face of the pressure plate and the withdrawal lever. The hole in the end of each withdrawal lever has two small slots diametrically opposed on each side of its periphery. Two projections on the nut that holds the assembly together register in these slots and the end of the bolt shank has a screwdriver slot cut in it so that adjustment to compensate for wear of the thrust ring is easily effected.

Each withdrawal lever is pivoted on a two-pronged lug pressed back from the rear cover. The prongs register in two slots punched in the lever. An open ended slot is cut in the inner end of the lever. In it is registered a tongue projecting from the front face of the circular plate, on the rear of which bears the carbon-type thrust ring. The circular plate is retained by three radially disposed hairpin-type springs, with looped inner ends which register in tangential

grooves in lugs extended radially from its periphery. These springs are coiled near their outer ends, which are sprung into holes in the rear cover.

The clutch control lever, its spindle and the two levers carrying the trunnion housing for the carbon-type thrust bearing are supplied in one piece. Assembly into the bellhousing is an unusually simple operation. The right-hand end of the spindle is shouldered to form a journal that is carried in a hole in the bellhousing. At the other end, the journal is formed by the boss of the control lever. A slot is machined horizontally from the front face of the bellhousing and breaks into the hole in which this boss is carried. The slot is of such a width that the spindle can be passed into it from the front; when this has been done, the spindle is moved to the right so that the boss on the left and the shouldered end on the right enter their bearings. The assembly is retained by a circlip in a groove round the right-hand end of the spindle.

On the ends of the two pendant levers on this spindle are semi-circular housings for the trunnions on each side of the carbon thrust-bearing. Each of these trunnions is retained in its housing by spring clip, and the two assemblies are carried in cradles at the pendant ends of a forked lever. This lever is centrally pivoted on a 9mm-diameter spindle; at its other end is the compression coil spring that acts on the lever to return the bearing clear of the thrust plate when the clutch is engaged. The spindle is located by a set screw in the lever, the end of the screw registering in a groove round the centre of the spindle. This method of holding the carbon thrust bearing appears to be rather insecure, but it apparently is satisfactory and has been adopted because of the restricted space available in front of the trunnions.

As is usual with front-wheel drive units, the final drive unit is located between the engine and gearbox. The drive is transmitted to the mainshaft by a long primary shaft, and the crown wheel of the spiral bevel, final drive unit is integral with the layshaft. Thus all gears are indirect. Ratios are: top 1.474:1, third 1.94:1, second 3.24:1, first 6.69:1 and reverse 7.26:1. All forward gears are engaged through synchromesh units and helical gears are employed for all except the first and reverse trains.

A common casing is employed for the final drive and gearbox, so the same lubricating oil is used for both; the capacity is 2.2 pints. The casing is in three pieces, the main part of the box being divided vertically in the plane containing the axes of the final drive shafts. Integral with the front portion is the bellhousing, which does not totally enclose the flywheel, but extends above and below it and is in effect a large bracket by means of which the transmission unit is attached to the engine. This leaves part of the flywheel and ring gear exposed so that, when the engine is running, care must be taken to avoid getting clothing caught in the moving parts.

The front and intermediate sections of the casing are held together by eight studs, all carried in the intermediate section of

*Neater late-type door handle.*

the box. The rear portion is little more than a cover on the back of the gearbox. However, it also locates the two-row ball-bearing that carries the tail end of the mainshaft, and the turret housing for the gear shift control is bolted on the top of it.

At the front end of the primary shaft are the eight splines that transmit the drive from the centre plate of the clutch. Behind these is an oil return scroll working in a bore in the front wall of the box. Immediately to the rear of this is a ball-bearing, also housed in the front wall. The bearing is inserted from the rear; its outer race is located against a collar machined integrally with the shaft.

A thread is machined on the periphery of this collar, which appears to be incorporated so that the nut securing the rear bearing can be used as an extractor for the inner race of the bearing. On assembly the nut is screwed past this collar and then slid along the waisted portion of the shaft and screwed on to the thread at the rear. It pulls the inner race of the rear ball-bearing against the primary gear, which has nineteen teeth and which is formed near the tail end of the shaft.

Location of the whole primary shaft assembly is effected at the outer race of the bearing which is housed in the intermediate web dividing the gearbox from the final drive casing. A snap ring in a groove round the periphery of the outer race is located against the front face of the web, and the whole assembly is secured by means of a ring on which are two diametrically opposed lugs drilled for two set-bolts screwed into the web. These set-bolts pull the ring against the outer race.

A short extension of the shaft behind the primary gear is a counterbore for the needle roller bearing that carries the front end of the mainshaft. This bearing is retained in its housing by a circlip in a groove in the bore. The rear end of the extension of the primary shaft has twelve splines machined on it in groups of four, and the centres of the groups are spaced 120 degrees apart. Between each group is a space, the width of which is approximately equivalent to that occupied by two teeth. Immediately in front of the splines is a groove cut round the shaft, and behind this is a collar in which three slots are cut. These slots are in line with the gaps between the groups of four splines. This arrangement on the end of the primary shaft forms the inner member of the synchro mechanism for the third speed gear.

The cone ring has three internal splines or teeth, spaced at 120 degrees apart, and it rides with its teeth in the spaces between the groups of four splines already mentioned. When the gear is selected, the cones are engaged and the cone ring slides forward. However, a spring ring of semi-circular cross-section, interposed between the three teeth and the slotted collar, temporarily prevents it from crossing the groove in the primary shaft extension. The leading edges of the three splines are chamfered so that they can compress the ring into the groove and ride over it into the three slots in the collar. One end of the spring ring is turned to the rear between the two splines on the primary shaft extension. Initially, the resistance offered by the spring ring to the axial motion of the core ensures that the outer cone, which is housed in the sliding member, is fully engaged to effect synchronization; the final axial motion of the internally splined sliding member locks together the mainshaft and primary shaft. This type of synchromesh mechanism is used for all four speeds, but there is no spring ring in the synchro arrangement serving bottom gear.

The bronze outer synchro cone is riveted in a counterbore in the front end of the sliding member. When it is withdrawn it comes up against a snapring in a groove round the

*Early type of window catch – a rubber bung which held the front window flap in the raised position.*

rear of the inner cone ring, which it pulls out of engagement. A similar synchro arrangement, for second speed gear, is incorporated in a counterbore at the rear end of the sliding member which is, of course, splined on the mainshaft. Round that end is the channel for the selector fork. This channel is screwed on and tightened against a set of splines for another sliding member, which is carried on the periphery of the one just described. The reason for screwing on the channel for the selector fork is that the splines could not otherwise be machined in the limited space available.

On the outer sliding member are the thirty-three teeth of a straight spur gear and the channel for the selector fork for first and reverse speeds. Housed in its front end is the cone ring for the first speed synchro mechanism. This mechanism is the same as the one previously described for fourth speed gear, except that there is no spring ring. This ring is omitted because, if it were not, there would be a danger of the inner and outer sliding members moving

forward simultaneously. Once the initial motion of the outer member has taken place and the interlock mechanism between the selector rods has come into action, there is no longer any danger of the centre portion and fourth and bottom gears being engaged simultaneously. The reason why the somewhat unusual practice of incorporating a synchro mechanism for bottom has been adopted is because the vehicle has such a low power-to-weight ratio that a change down into bottom is frequently necessary to ascend steep hills.

Floating on the mainshaft, immediately behind the splines for the two sliding members of the synchro units, is the helical second speed gear. The splines, groove and collar of the synchro mechanism are machined round its forward extended boss. A nut on the rear end of the mainshaft is tightened against an assembly comprising the speedometer gear, a conical distance piece, the two inner races of a two-row ball bearing, and a sixteen-toothed helical gear which is splined on the shaft. This gear is pulled against a shoulder on the shaft, and a distance tube is interposed between it and the floating second speed gear. It is in constant mesh with a sixteen-toothed gear splined on the layshaft and transmits the drive for all speeds except top. The whole mainshaft assembly is located by a flange round the rear end of the outer race of the rear bearing, which is clamped between the rear cover and the end wall of the gearbox.

The rear end of the layshaft is carried in a two-row ball bearing, the two inner races of which are pulled by a nut against the splined-on gear. This gear, in turn, is pulled against a shoulder on the shaft. The flanged outer race is retained by a plate secured by four 7mm-diameter studs in the rear wall of the box, against which it clamps the flange. Machined on the periphery of a forward extension of the boss of the gear are the splines, groove and collar round which is the inner cone of the fourth speed synchro mechanism. The phosphor bronze outer cone differs from the others in that, instead of being riveted to the sliding member, it is pressed into it.

A groove for the selector fork is machined on the sliding member, which is carried on an externally splined rearward extension of the layshaft cluster. The layshaft cluster is carried on two phosphor bronze bushes, one at each end. They are lubricated through radial holes in their housings. Two thrust washers are used, one between the rear of the cluster and the layshaft gear, and the other between the front of the cluster and the two-row ball bearing supporting that end of the shaft. There are four gears on the cluster.

Between the rear end of the cluster and the spiral bevel final drive pinion is the inner race of the two-row ball-bearing already mentioned. The outer race of this race is floating in its housing in the intermediate web of the gearbox. Adjustment of the axial position of the shaft is effected by shims interposed between the inner race of the rear bearing and the gear in front of it.

Carried in the top of the box are the three selector rods. A conventional spring-loaded ball arrangement, housed in vertical drillings in the rear wall of the gearbox and final drive casing, engages in a groove beneath each rod to form the gear lock mechanism. The gear interlock mechanism is housed in the intermediate web of the box. It consists of two balls in the spaces between the rods and a third underneath the centre one. The balls between the rods register in grooves in the sides of the rods, while the third is spring-loaded into a groove under the centre rod. The relative dimensions of the grooves and balls are such that, when the centre rod is moved axially to select a gear, it forces the balls on each side of it into the grooves in the side rods. When one of the side rods is moved, it forces the adjacent ball into engagement with a groove in the centre rod.

The striker rods are formed integrally on the rear ends of the rods which overhang into the rear cover of the gearbox. A casting bolted on top of this cover houses the striker lever at the base of the gearshift control. A conventional ball-and-socket mounting is employed for this control: the ball is spring-loaded upwards into its socket. Spring-loaded plungers on each side of the striker pre-load it to the central position. A peg inserted from the rear of the cover forms a baulk stop to prevent movement of the lever directly from the first and reverse speed fork into the top-speed one, and vice versa. This peg is of such a length that it is necessary to change into third speed before moving into fourth and back again into third speed before engaging second speed. The selector forks for fourth, third and second speeds have split bosses through which the rods are threaded and they are each clamped with a set screw. The fork for reverse and first speeds is similarly mounted on the rod, but is secured by two set screws.

At the upper end of the gearshift lever is a fork end in which a cranked rod is pinned. From the fork end, this rod is extended a short distance to the rear; it is then bent downwards and again to the rear where it is carried in an almost horizontal tube mounted under the dash. The other end of the rod, where it protrudes from the end of this tube, is bent up and tipped by a knob. Moving the control knob from side to side moves the lever mounted on top of the gearbox likewise. Similarly, pull and push motions applied to the knob move the gear lever backwards and forwards.

## FINAL DRIVE

A final drive of simple design is employed, housed in a casing which is divided in the transverse, vertical plane. The swinging portions of the half shafts are inclined rearwards so that the suspension crosstube can pass behind the gearbox.

The crown wheel is spigoted on the left side of the one-piece differential cage. It is secured by six set bolts fitted with one locking plate to each pair of bolts. One of these bolts has a dowel extension on the end of its shank. This extension registers in a hole in the spindle for the two differential pinions.

Two flats are machined on the periphery of the spindle to feed oil outwards into the journal bearings of the pinions. These pinions each have ten teeth and their flat outer faces bear directly on the cage. The differential wheels have sixteen teeth and eight internal splines. On the left side, the boss of the differential wheel is carried in the boss of the crown wheel, while that on the right is in the cage. The flat outer faces of the differential gears bear at one side on the crown wheel and at the other, on the cage.

Two taper roller bearings, each housed in the two parts of the final drive casing, carry the final drive gear assembly. The inner race

*Late rear lamp cluster with revised bumper style.*

of the bearing on the left is on the shouldered end of the crown wheel boss, while the bearing on the other side is similarly located against a shoulder on the differential cage. Adjustment of the preload of these bearings is effected by shims interposed between the outer races and the castings that form the back pleats of the front brakes. The bearings for the half shafts are housed in these castings, which are spigoted into the final drive casing and secured by six studs, and nut-locked with spring washers.

The inner ends of the half shafts are splined into the differential wheels, while each outer end is carried in a single-row ball bearing. A ring nut screwed into each housing from the inner end pulls the outer race of the bearing against a shoulder in the casting. This ring nut is slotted to receive a locking peg driven through a hole in the casting. Another nut is screwed on to the half shaft to pull the inner race of the bearing against a shoulder on the shaft. Immediately outboard of this shoulder is a lip-type oil seal that bears on the shaft and which is assembled into its housing from the outer end. A fork of the universal joint is formed on the outer end of the half-shaft. A thrower ring is machined round the base of the fork. It is completely enshrouded by a channel-section ring pressed on to the oil seal housing. Thus, any lubricant leaking past the seal is thrown into this ring, at the bottom of which is fitted a pipe that drains it away through a hole in the back plate. A shouldered flange is formed immediately outboard of the thrower to carry the spigoted-on brake drum secured by four studs and nuts.

Conventional needle roller bearing-type universal joints are used at both ends of each swinging half shaft. It is not considered necessary to use constant velocity joints for this vehicle, because of its low-rated engine and limited maximum speed. (However, snatch on tight corners at low speed necessitated putting in the clutch to prevent tyre scrub and loss of adhesion. Later, when engines became more powerful, Citroen did indeed use constant velocity joints here.)

The sleeve of the sliding joint is incorporated with the outer fork of the inner universal joint. One of the forks of the outer universal joint is formed integrally with the inner member of the sliding joint and the other is on the splined driving shaft. This shaft is threaded at its outer end for the castellated nut that pulls the wheel hub on to it.

A two-row ball bearing with a single outer race and two inner races is carried round the inboard end of the hub. The inner races of this bearing are clamped between a shoulder on the hub and the fork of the universal joint on the driving shaft. Its outer race is pulled against a shoulder in the swivel-pin carrier forging by means of a ring nut screwed into the forging from the inner end. This ring nut also acts as the housing for the lip-type oil seal at that end. The oil seal bears on a collar, formed round the driving shaft, adjacent to the fork of the universal joint. Another lip-type oil seal is inserted from the other end into the swivel pin carrier forging and bears on the wheel hub. Outboard of this seal, the hub is flanged and carries the three 12mm-diameter studs that secure the wheels.

**STEERING SYSTEM**

The 17mm-diameter swivel pin is carried in two knuckles on an extension of the forging that forms the housing for the wheel hub and driving shaft assembly. Bearings are of phosphor bronze and are spaced 64mm apart, as measured between the adjacent ends of the bushes. A small forged boss between the two knuckles is spigoted and welded in the end of the tubular suspension arm. Between the lower face of the boss and the upper face of the lower bearing knuckle is a shrouded three-washer-type thrust bearing. The outer pair of washers are of steel and the centre one of bronze.

A pressed-on domed cap seals the upper end of the top knuckle. The lower end of the bottom knuckle is sealed by a bolted-on steel plate and a joint washer. In the centre of this plate is a grease nipple. The lubricant is passed from the nipple up an axial hole in the swivel pin and through radial holes to the bushes. In some models, one radial hole serves each bush; in others, two are provided. One end of the steering lever registers in a slot in the top of the forging that carries the wheel hub assembly. It is held down in the slot by two bolts. The other end of this lever forms the centre component of a ball-and-socket joint. The halves of the spherical bearings in the socket are spring-loaded to provide self-adjustment for wear.

The steering arrangement is a conventional rack-and-pinion layout with a three-piece track rod. At the outer end of each of the two end rods are the ball-and-socket joints mentioned before. An eye in the inner end of each rod carries a ball fitting for another ball-and-socket joint. The ball is on a stem tapered and keyed into the eye, and retained by a slotted nut; two diametrically opposed flats are machined on it, so that it can be passed through a relatively small slot in the font face of the socket. The socket is a tube spun over a head up-ended on the rack, and is self-adjusting for wear.

The rack-and-pinion assembly is housed in the crosstube that carries the pivots of the suspension arms. Bolted inside the front of this tube is a pressed steel housing for the ball-and-socket end of the rack. A spherical bearing-ring is riveted round the socket tube to reduce the friction between it and the pressed steel housing. During assembly, the rack is passed through a slot in the front face of the crosstube. This slot also provides the necessary clearance for the ball fittings to move from side-to-side with the rack. It is closed by a plate that is mounted on and moves with the ball fittings. This plate is spring-loaded against the crosstube. The other end of the track is carried in the pinion housing which is welded inside the crosstube.

A spring-loaded plunger underneath the rack forces it into engagement with the pinion, which has seven helical teeth. This plunger is retained in its housing by a cupped plug that is screwed in and locked by a split pin. Two bearings support the pinion shaft, which is only 107mm long. The lower bearing is of the bush type. A domed steel plug is pressed into the bottom end of its housing to retain the lubricant and keep out the dust. The upper bearing is of the ball type. Its outer race is retained in the housing by a ring nut, and the inner race is formed by a groove round the shaft. A felt sealing ring in a cupped shroud is housed in the ring nut. Immediately above this, the shaft is splined into the tubular steering column. Axial location is effected by a bolt clamping a split ring round the tube. The shank of this bolt registers in a groove round the splined portion of the shaft. Turning circle is 35ft 6in to the left and 35ft 3in to the right.

## CHASSIS FRAME AND BRAKES

The stub axle for each rear wheel is welded in its suspension arm, and the pressed steel brake back plate is welded on to it. Outboard of the back plate, the axle is shouldered for the two-row ball-bearing that carries the wheel hub. This bearing has a single outer race and a two-piece inner race. The inner race is pulled on by a nut on the end of the stub axle, and the outer race is retained in its housing by a ring nut

*The instruction book illustration showing the use of the wood 'scotch' used to chock the diagonally opposite wheel before jacking the car. This oak or beech scotch was included in the toolkit of every 2CV.*

screwed into the outer end of the hub. A domed cap pressed into the ring nut retains the grease and prevents ingress of dust. A lip-type oil seal is housed in the inner end of the hub, and bears on the stub axle. The wheel is secured by three nuts and studs to a flange round the hub. These studs, which have round heads up-ended at their inner ends, serve to secure the brake drum to the inner face of the flange.

Lockheed hydraulic leading and trailing shoe brakes are fitted both at front and rear. The drum diameter is 8.87in and shoe width 1.55in. Shoe area is 31.4sq in at the front and 30.8sq in at the rear. The handbrake is of the pistol-grip type and operates on the front wheels. This allows a short cable to be used, which is an advantage financially, and makes the operation more positive.

The frame is of exceptionally rigid design and measures 3,540mm (11ft 7.5in). Rigidity is of far more importance to the quality of ride than is normally realized. A flexible frame tends to give the occupants of the vehicle a subconscious sense of insecurity when the vehicle traverses anything but smooth ground. The vague uneasiness experienced is interpreted by the conscious mind into a feeling that the whole structure is unstable, and that the ride is not all it might be.

Over the whole length of the chassis, the side members of the frame are straight. They are of box section, formed by two channel sections with their flanges extended outwards. One is shallow and is placed inside the other, which is of deeper section. The flanges of the shallow one are turned outwards through 180 degrees and are wrapped round the flanges of the deeper one, to which they are spot welded. This strengthens the flange enough to carry the suspension crosstubes. Over the centre portion of the frame, the inner channel at each side is cranked inwards to form a kind of cruciform bracing over the length between the front and rear suspension crosstubes. The centre parallel portions of the cranked member on each side are 8in apart and are parallel for a distance of 2ft 11in.

Between points immediately in front of the front suspension crosstube and behind the rear one, the whole of the frame is completely boxed in by closing plates welded on top of, and below, the side members and cruciform members. Spot welding is employed for the junction of the plate to the cruciform members, and at the outer edges of the plate where it is carried in the 180-degree bend of the flange of the shallow channel, to which it is spot welded. An indication of the width of the frame can be gained from the fact that the distance between the pairs of bolt holes drilled in the flanges of the side members for mounting the suspension crosstubes is 556mm, or around 22in.

At the rear, the ends of the top and bottom plates are cut back towards the centre in a semi-circular fashion between the side members, and the end is closed by a channel section, the flanges of which extend rearwards and are spot welded to the plates. A similar arrangement is employed at the front, but the lower plate is extended forwards under the cross member beneath the gearbox. This cross member is of top hat section, and its flanges are welded to the extension of the bottom plate. Its top face is extended on each side to overlap the frame side members to which it is welded. Between this cross member and the semi-circular channel that closes the front end of the centre portion of the frame, louvres are punched in the bottom plate for drainage purposes.

At the forward end of the frame, there is another box section cross member formed by a top hat section with a closing plate welded to its flanges, which are at the front. The top and bottom walls of this section are extended on each side to overlap the side members, to which they are welded. There are no cross members at the rear of the frame, but two tubular ones in the boxed-in portion between the suspension crosstubes are passed through the side members and the cruciform member. They are spaced with their axes 597mm (23.5in) apart, and they overhang each side of the frame far enough to carry the suspension spring assembly. Top hat-section outrigger extensions are welded on top of them to carry the body. The outer ends of each of these outriggers on each side are spaced apart by another top hat section welded on. This forms the body sill and supports the front seat.

The occasional incredulity of the engineers who prepared this report is leavened by the obvious admiration they have for the mechanical solutions sought in the pursuit of exiguity by Pierre Boulanger's team.

# 4   The 2CV in Production

The launch of the 2CV at the 1948 Paris Motor Show was greeted with not a little derision by the motoring press of the day. One American wag asked if the car was supplied with a can-opener, while the *Autocar* commented, 'The designer has kissed the lash of austerity with almost masochistic fervour.' It was only after the car had been in production for a few years that *The Motor* was kind enough to comment that the 2CV was a 'vehicle with almost every virtue except speed, silence and good looks'.

*The 1948 Paris Motor Show where the 2CV made its public appearance. Guards were placed by each car to prevent the curious public from lifting bonnets or rocking the body to see how the suspension worked. Arranged just across the aisle is Renault's display of its 4CV model, which just beat the 2CV into production.*

The sceptical press did not notice, perhaps, that during the show some 1,300,000 French people visited the three 2CVs on the Citroën stand and thousands of orders were placed for the car, which was not to appear for another year. A guard was needed to prevent visitors trying to open the bonnets which had been sealed, and to stop them from bouncing the little car to observe its innovative suspension units at either side.

True to Pierre Boulanger's original idea for the future buyers of the car, Citroën vetted the potential purchasers to ensure they were of the favoured professions for which the car was designed. The list for the first cars and a couple of years later for the Fourgonnette van (*see* pages 100–3) included farmers, commercial travellers, pastrycooks, milliners, bakers, electricians, florists, drapers, chemists, shoemakers, hoteliers, grocers, painters, radio service agents, interior decorators, glaziers, mercery dealers and artificial inseminators! If you weren't in the list, Citroën took your name but it could take years to get to the top of the waiting list. At one point this was six years. Boulanger had originally intended the 2CV as a vehicle for country people to use, but the post-war situation helped Citroën to impose the list of favoured professions.

Immediately post-war, supplies of steel were difficult to get and soon after the Paris Motor Show it was clear that Citroën couldn't get adequate supplies to meet demand. Since supply was limited, it was logical that the possible outlets were filtered by means of the list, so that the cars would reach the people for whom they were originally intended. Citroën could easily have sold more than three times the number of cars they could actually make.

To bring the Citroën 2CV into production, the design of the body had to be modified to make volume production possible, by a Maurice Steck of the *Méthodes Technique* department. Throughout its history the 2CV has been subject to improvements and changes, many of which were to the first production cars delivered in November 1949 from the show cars. Many of these changes were due to the rationalization of the bodywork for production and included changes to the rear wings and bonnet: construction involved the minimum of press-tooling, and from the first cars until the last, the 2CV was always a labour-intensive car to make. The ignition system, side windows, door handles and details to the hood fixings were also all fine-tuned before the cars entered production.

*A pre-production 2CV – perhaps one of the 1948 Paris Motor Show cars. A number of changes would identify the actual production cars. None of those had the slanting grille bars visible on this one.*

The production history of the 2CV is complicated enough that a basic précis of the various models made over the years is worth noting. There were many variants, not counting the non-French specials built for specific markets. The first model was the A-type, built from 1948–61. Then came the AZ, built from 1954–61, which spawned four subsequent models: the AZL of 1956–70, the AZLP of 1957–63, the AZA of 1963–70 and the AZAM of 1963–70. From 1961 to 1970 a hatchback version was built, at first called the AZC or *Mixte* and then later the AZL or AZAM *Commerciale*. The AZL 4 (or AZ series AZ) and AZL 6 (or AZ series KA) were introduced in 1970. It is entirely likely that the works descriptions of any of the above models may bear different symbols, letters and numbers, as Citroën has never been the most logical company in the area of model names.

## THE A-TYPE

The 2CV 'Citroën Cabriolet', as originally launched in France, was an inspired work of automotive economy. The new owners would take delivery of a four-door, four-light saloon with all non-essential equipment eliminated to save weight and cost, keeping total weight to under half a ton and cost (in 1953) to FF341,870 – about £350. The roof and luggage compartment were covered by a roll-back hood; the roof section could be fastened in any of three positions. The rear windscreen was supported within the fixed section of this continuous hood material. The corrugated bonnet enclosed the engine bay and had slats at the bonnet sides to aid air-cooling and a large slatted grille inside which was an oval trim enclosing the double chevron Citroën symbol. Below this was the

*Perhaps this was how the majority of 2CVs were used, muddy and plugging up a dirt track.*

hole for the starting handle and below that the bonnet lock handle. Headlamps were affixed to a single bar which ran transversely through the front of the bonnet. At the rear there was a single tail light and a single stop light, and the number plate was illuminated by a centrally located lamp shining to either side. The whole car was finished in a darkish metallic grey and there were no colour options.

Doors were hinged at the centre of the car, front doors opening from the front and rear doors from the rear. Only the front doors had opening windows, which comprised of a section which hinged up and clipped in the open position. Seats could easily be removed to double as chairs. The floor covering was rubber matting and the door insides were trimmed with a simple board covering. Seats were constructed from tubular steel and had canvas coverings supported on rubber tension springs, leaving the under-seat area free for storage. The rear seats could be removed in seconds by releasing a single spring clip, to provide extra space for luggage stowage, or to provide picnic seating.

The controls were simplicity itself and instrumentation was kept to a minimum. An ammeter sat in front of the driver, forward of the two-spoked steering wheel. Two controls on this pod were for the choke and starter, with the ignition key switch to the side. The lights and horn were controlled by a now common but then revolutionary steering column stalk. A speedometer was provided which also provided the drive for the windscreen wipers, the disadvantage being that the slower the car goes, the slower the wipers go. A bit of a menace in slow-moving city streets, but Citroën provided them with a manual control as well, and it was at least a more sensible system than the vacuum wipers of many cars of the Fifties, which went very slowly when the car was travelling fast and speeded up as the car slowed down! No instrument lighting was provided. Fresh air was provided by a scuttle panel below the windscreen which could be screwed open and shut, and was protected by a gauze to exclude insects. A simple heater drew warm air from the cooling ducts on the engine cylinders. A small handwheel under the facia enabled the driver to adjust

*Alloy front wing 'spats' were made by many manufacturers as after-sale fitments. They protect those parts of the wings most prone to road spray, and from the occupants' feet when entering.*

*The two-horse mascot on the bonnet is an after-sale but period add-on to this 1961 AZL.*

the angle of headlamp beam, which alters with the car's load. A full-width parcel shelf gave room for oddments; below this was situated the umbrella-handle handbrake.

The petrol tank was provided with an accurate dipstick which was stored beside the filler neck, telling when the 4.4gal tank needed filling. Access to the engine bay was about as good as it gets: the front wings could be removed in moments with the use of the wheelbrace and the bonnet could be removed by slackening two thumbscrews. Standard kit included a clip-on cover for the grille to maintain heat in cold conditions and the wooden 'scotch' or wheel block – an essential item for use on the diagonally opposite wheel when changing wheels. The two-cylinder 375cc engine of square

dimensions gave 9bhp at 3500rpm and a top speed of about 40mph on the level. Fuel consumption averaged better than 60mpg. From October 1954 a higher capacity 425cc engine became available, raising power to 12bhp. However, the smaller engine was still available until 1959. Drum brakes all round, inboard at the front, gave excellent stopping power for this light car at light pedal pressure. Rack-and-pinion steering was accurate on the standard Michelin radial tyres.

The Slough-built models that entered production in 1953 differed from French ones in a few ways. The luggage locker was not considered secure with its fabric covering so a simple metal door hinged at the top was fitted to give the luggage some security.

The canvas seat covering was also changed to plastic. A large fore-and-aft-mounted mascot proclaiming 'Front Drive' was affixed to the bonnet, and it has been said that this massive Mazak casting slowed the 2CV's top speed a notch! Script-type Citroën badges were also fixed to the bonnet side and to the rear luggage door. These were taken directly from the Traction Avant. At the front the elliptical ring around the double-chevron Citroën logo on the grille was deleted for the Slough versions. Rear lamp lenses also had the Citroën chevrons moulded into the plastic. More fundamental changes were the addition of opening windows in the rear doors and chromium-plated bumpers. Inside an interior light fixed to the top rail shone directly onto the speedometer for night driving; it was fitted with a shroud that could be turned to provide lighting to the interior.

From the beginning the gearbox was all-synchromesh and contributed to the 2CV's ease of operation, but with the 1954 cars came the addition of a centrifugal clutch as standard, making stop-go driving much easier for the operator; clutchless gearchanges could be made with ease. On starting, first or second gear is selected and the accelerator is actuated as if the car had a fluid flywheel – the centrifugal weights act at about 1,000rpm. Once on the move the clutch can be ignored if the driver has time to spare: as the engine revs must drop below the speed at which the clutch bites before gearchanges can be made, in the upper ratios this can be a considerable time and a distinct loss in road speed would result, so it is better to use the clutch for speed of gearchanging. From 1961 the centrifugal clutch became an optional rather than standard feature. The simple Hookes joints fitted to the drive shafts – in place of the more commonplace constant velocity joints – did produce some steering wheel snatch on tight

turns. It proved advisable to slip the clutch to prevent this.

From 1955 an improved piston design with a 5mm domed centre gave a higher compression ratio and slightly more power, to 12.5bhp. Engines also ran faster, to 4200rpm. The last AZ model in 1962/3 could manage 15bhp with an improved carburettor and a 7.5:1 compression ratio.

The first refinements – if at this stage they could be described thus – came in December 1950 when an ignition key was fitted to the right side of the instrument panel. Door latches were also fitted with a key lock. October 1952 saw a new colour scheme: an even darker grey but with yellow wheels and again, no options. The spring-loaded bonnet catch of the first cars was replaced by a turn handle in May 1953 and in June that year the engine fan was changed from three- to four-bladed to increase efficiency. The twin bonnet supports were replaced by a single, stronger, one and the welded, hand-made construction of the bonnet and doors was dropped in favour of the much quicker all-pressed versions. Cars made by the early welded method can be identified by welded seams at the sides.

## THE AZ

The new AZ model appeared in September 1954 with a host of improvements, not least of which was the new 425cc engine giving 12bhp with an increase in maximum speed from 43mph to 49mph. Bore and stroke were identical to the 375cc engine, as was compression ratio. A different Solex carburettor was fitted and the engine fan now had six blades. While the gearbox was identical to that of the A-type, the transmission now incorporated a centrifugal clutch unique to the AZ model. This made driving around town much easier as the clutch had hardly to be used at all. The elliptical surround to the grille chevrons disappeared and indicator flashers were fitted high up on the rear three-quarter panels, while twin stop lights were fitted at the rear. The hinged door glasses could now be held in place by a rubber clasp at the top of the door frame. Interior trim was offered in more than the one grey colour: a dark green material with red and yellow squares was offered along with a plaid or checked pattern predominantly blue in colour. Exterior colour, however, remained the same. The speedometer was replaced by one with clear numbers, but it was still mounted on the screen pillar.

*Adrian Oldfield's 1961 AZL shows the amazing engine bay accessibility with the bonnet raised.*

Controls for the turn signals and the sidelights were fitted to a plate extending each side of the upper edge of the instrument panel. Some water leaks on earlier models prompted Citroën to improve things by adding drain tubes to the scuttle in January 1956, and by an improved seal along the join of the hinged side windows in April.

It was now clear that the 2CV was a definite success and had filled a gap in the market. That market, however, was changing. It was increasingly obvious that the motoring public were beginning to expect more from a car, even an economy model like the 2CV. So in December 1956, appearing alongside the A and AZ types, came the AZL the L signifying the works identification of *Luxe* – luxury.

Although mechanically identical to the AZ models, the AZL looked a bit smarter with trim strips along the bottom of the body and down the centre of the bonnet. The Citroën name appeared in the centre of the rear bumper, which was improved with a trim strip. The steering wheel, seat frames and gear knob were painted a lighter grey than the bodywork and this colour was continued on the outside where the wheels and bumpers painted in this colour relieved the unchanged dark grey of the bodywork. New upholstery in three colours, blue, red or green, was matched by the colour of the hood, which was now of a synthetic plastic in place of the original canvas. Rear vision was improved with a larger rear window. Controls improvements included placing the indicator turn switch in the centre of the dashboard and incorporating a demister/defroster, operating on the driver's side only.

The locking metal bootlid developed by the Slough team did not appear on a French model until September 1957 when a further model, the AZLP appeared. This model also had a central number plate and lamp at the rear and was slightly more expensive than the other models.

When the demisting duct was made larger in 1959, it came with controls to open the heater ducts and an improved interior heater. At last in September 1959 came a colour option: Glacier Blue with a blue hood and seats. The grey was of course still available! Different tyres were available at the 135 × 380 size and for the first time a

Citroën-designed radio – the Radioën – could be fitted. This fairly huge device fitted under the screen on the passenger side and took up most of the parcel shelf space. One could be forgiven for thinking that Citroën's colour stylists had gone mad when another two exterior colours appeared in September and December 1960: Panama

*This 1961 AZL shows the new bonnet, which had appeared in 1960.*

*The rear end shows the divided number plate and small lamps.*

(Above) *Fluted bonnets like this remained until 1960.*

(Left) *This French AZL has the optional extra of the extended pressed steel bootlid for added capacity. With it came a different rear bumper.*

Yellow and Spray Green could be had with either green or brown interiors. These subtle changes had now added up to something of a complete redesign in 1960 with the change from the original corrugated bonnet to one lacking the louvred side panels and having only five, wider spaced, flutes running front to back. The through-flow of air was provided by indented side panels to the engine bay and fixed to the wing of the car, rather than to the bonnet itself. This much neater approach gave a cleaner look to the 2CV, but the home handyman could still have the superb access to the engine bay by removing these panels, which only took a few minutes. The bonnet itself locked automatically when closed and a new grille completed the facelift. Minor improvements at this time included a new clip to hold the door glass open and redesigned seat frames. Two new types of material for the seats appeared in July 1961. More importantly, the choice of transmission could be either standard or centrifugal clutch, while reinforced door and bonnet locks were fitted to all models. October 1961 saw Poppy Red as an additional exterior colour for the AZLP, complemented by either dark grey or brown hoods.

March 1962 saw the arrival of the AZC or *Mixte* model as a sort of halfway house between the Fourgonnette vans and the saloons. Just as the Traction Avant had been offered with hatchback-type bootlids which included the rear window, so was the 2CV offered with this enlarged bootlid for accepting larger loads. In other respects the car remained the same as the AZLP, but hinged above the rear window. The spare wheel was fitted under the bonnet, and the rear seat could be folded forward out of the way. A ribbed floor in the rear made it both stronger and able to withstand rougher use. These models were called either AZC or the ENAC – after the company which was subcontracted to do the conversions for Citroën.

By September 1962 the original buyers of 1950 would still have recognized the car, but they would have been stunned by its increased sophistication. Instrumentation now included a fuel gauge, ammeter and a speedometer with trip gauge mounted on the instrument panel, rather than on the windscreen pillar. Windscreen wipers had their own electric motor rather than sharing the

drive with the old speedometer cable. Seats were now available in brown and mandarin.

AZLP production ceased in February 1963 when this model was replaced by the AZA which, although identical from the outside, differed in many mechanical details. The gearbox and final drive unit had revised ratios and gave a higher top speed of 59mph with the slightly uprated

(Above) *From December 1964 all models featured doors hinged at the front. This example – an AZA or AZAM – also features the side-mounted indicators, identifying it as a French-built model.*

*This 1966 AZAM model was the first incarnation of the six-light French models providing a lighter appearance to the rear end. This model also sported the new three-bar grille.*

engine giving 18bhp at 5,000rpm, while stopping power was provided by improved bonded brake shoes in place of the old riveted type. Another new model was launched in March 1963, called the AZAM – apparently from the description of the new model as *ameliorée* (improved). It sported tubular chromed overriders, twin stoplights at the rear, chromed headlamp retaining rings and wiper arms, and smaller polished alloy door handles on the outside, while inside the door release handles were given plastic levers. Also different was the addition of stainless trim strips on the bonnet, stainless surrounds to the front windows and further bright trims to the front and rear screens.

Improvements continued inside with fore-and-aft adjustment of the front seat being made possible by mounting the seat on runners. The plain and simple horizontal-spoked steering wheel was now gone and replaced by one whose twin spokes formed a downward facing 'V'. The indicator switch was moved again, to just under the new steering wheel. The passenger got a sunvisor fitted with a vanity mirror, and the door trim panels were given a leather-look finish. At the rear a parcel shelf increased storage. New interior

colours of blue, brown, green and red were available, together with improved seat covers and better seat springing.

Seat belts were fitted for the first time in January 1964, to AZA and AZAM models, and this required a modification to the seats themselves to accept the lap-type belts. Still on the subject of safety, the front 'suicide' doors were altered to hinge from their leading edges after new safety regulations came into force in December 1964. In April, all models received a round identification plate to signify the exterior paint colour used on the bodywork. Tubeless tyres were also available from June 1964, and in July the flexible brake pipes and fittings of the ID and DS models were fitted to the AZA and AZAM, and the AZU Fourgonnette van. Gearbox casings became a pressure-flow casting for some models.

From September 1964 the colours available were revised for the AZA and AZAM. These were Agave Green, Slate Blue, Rose Grey and Typhoon Grey. In November 1964, the final drive bevel and pinion ratio was altered to 8:29 with a consequent revision of gearbox ratios. January 1965 saw a change to the gearbox selection forks in some gearboxes.

*The 1966 'Commerciale' Mixte was produced by the ENAC company and featured a bigger rear opening incorporating the rear window. It also had a tougher ribbed floor at the rear for the extra expected wear.*

July 1965 saw some more *amelioration* between the AZL ENAC and AZAM ENAC models, with a stronger framework at the rear and an improved support for the spare wheel. A more comfortable rear seat was fitted with an easier method of folding it down and attaching it in the upright position. The parking lights disappeared and their switch was used instead to operate two interior lights.

A new grille appeared in September 1965 with the double chevron Citroën symbol now affixed to the bonnet above a new, stronger-looking three-slatted cast stainless grille. Also different was the provision of a third window in the 'boxy' rear three-quarter, making the interior brighter and rearward visibility better. Bumpers were fitted with black plastic inserts on the main bar and overriders. Front wheel drive transmission joints were changed from simple universal joints to constant velocity joints. This improvement eliminated the snatch on tight corners at low speed, where with the earlier joints it had been advisable to slip the clutch around the corner.

In September 1965 the rear suspension dampers were replaced by hydraulic shock absorbers, while the suspension pots themselves gained waterproof rubber gaiters. An optional Gurtner independent interior heater became available. Meanwhile, the exterior colour revisions continued, this time to consist of Fog Blue, Etna Grey, Rose Grey and Agave Green. From May 1966 new door handles were fitted, together with new driver and passenger window retaining catches. Bucket seats were an option as was a Simplex anti-theft device and Bufflon vinyl trim. Exterior colours were now Danay Grey, Cyclades Blue and Agave Green.

## NEW MODELS FOR THE 1970s

There were very few changes in the next few years, which is perhaps explained by the appearance in 1970 of a new range supplanting the old AZA and AZAM models. While the old fabric-booted AZL base model was still available in Germany and Holland

*This shot of a 1967 AZAM4 shows the blissfully simple interior. The bulge above the gear-lever houses the wiper motor.*

– at least for a while – the 2CV range lost the commercial or *Mixte* model, now that the Dyane (*see* page 91) offered the hatch-back type of body. The two new models became known as the 2CV4 and 2CV6 – Citroën described them as the AZL4 and AZL6 at the factory. The 2CV4 had the 435cc engine – which had first seen light of day in the Dyane – while the 2CV6 had the engine first introduced for the Ami-6 in 1961. This was a 602cc engine which pushed it into the realms of 3CV for taxation, though it still retained its 2CV name. This engine used a full-flow oil filter of the replaceable canister type. The new models had all the improve-ments of the latest AZAM models together with a windscreen washer and steering lock as standard and the improved stainless steel window surrounds and adjustable front seat. Options available were the cen-trifugal clutch transmission, separate front seats and front seat-belts. Standard equip-ment included the AZAM-type black steer-ing wheel, rear-view door mirrors and a more comprehensive instrument panel, while cloth seat coverings could be specified in place of the Targa type.

The new cars had indicator lamps set into the front wings and larger composite rear lamps which obviated the need for the indi-cator lamps set high on the rear quarter-pil-lars of earlier models. New exterior colours were Swan White, Maple Beige, Masséna Red and Thasos Blue. The new models were badged on the bootlid with either 2CV4 or 2CV6. Pedals for the brake and clutch were of the suspended type, and reinforced from September 1971. From January 1972 the seat belts were of the three-point fixing diagonal and lap belt-type dictated by the new regulations imposed in some export markets. For the first time the belt was anchored on the central door pillar.

In September 1972 the cars received sound-deadening material on the front bulkhead and around the pedals, while the engine bay itself received some sound proof-ing. Stronger locks of the anti-burst type were also fitted for safety. Specifications note that both the new engines conformed to the new European anti-pollution legisla-tion. New colours appeared almost every year from now on: those for the 1973 season were Camargue Blue, Albatross Beige, Rio Red and 'Ivoire Borely'.

The 1974 season cars received a bigger brake master cylinder, reinforced rack-and-pinion steering components and an improved battery clamp to prevent the bat-tery sliding about. On the body, new metal badges at the rear denoted 2CV4 or 2CV6. The brown finish dashboard incorporated a new design of ashtray and the brown colour was continued onto the direction indicator and lamp stalk housings. The steering wheel of the 2CV6 was now the *monobranche* in leather-grained brown polypropylene, in line with the more expensive cars in the Citroën range. The Albatross Beige and Camargue Blue exte-rior colours were dropped – it doesn't mat-ter how you define it, beige is still beige! They were supplanted by Lagoon Blue, Palm Green and Tenerife Orange, with assorted colours for the hood.

The 1975 season cars (from September 1974) all had new rectangular headlamps to replace the round ones and a new plastic grille set higher, with the Citroën chevrons set into it. Rear bumpers were wider with a wide black plastic rubbing strip, and inside doors received a plastic band at the top of the door casings. Beige was back again, this time as Vanneau or Lapwing Beige, the other colours being Petrel Blue and Tuileries Green. Engines received an improved air fil-ter made of polymethane foam in a plastic casing enclosed in a new cover. Alterations to the hood fixings, with two interior hooks, meant that it could be retained in the half-

*Rectangular headlamps, as fitted to this 1974 model, were not popular. The 2CV returned to round lamps later.*

open position. A new Solex 34 PICS6 carburettor was fitted to the 2CV6 in two types, marked 164 for the ordinary clutch version and 165 for the centrifugal clutch version.

A simplified version based on the 2CV4 appeared in late 1975, named the 2CV Spécial. Back came the round headlamps of the pre-1974 models, while the body returned to a four-light configuration. The hood was of the older type without the sophistication of the new hood catches, and inside the fittings were all of more meagre specifications. A 2CV Spécial badge was fixed to the bootlid and the Spécial was only available in Cedrat Yellow. There were no aluminium trim strips on the rear wings and doors.

The 2CV6 received a revised steering ratio and the steering wheel was consequently reduced in diameter, while the suspension was improved with shock absorbers replacing the old-type cylinder-and-weight system. Both the standard 2CV4 and 2CV6 were fitted with adhesive strips to the bumpers in place of the rubber strips – definitely a retrograde step. Seat belts were improved with semi-flexible stalk-type fixings in the middle of the car. The Cedrat Yellow of the Spécial was joined by Bamboo Green as new colours for both models in addition to the last season's colours.

In April 1976 a limited edition – apparently of 1,800 examples – appeared, the 2CV

Spot. This had eye-catching orange and white two-tone paintwork, square headlamps and the Spot logo on the side stripes crossing the front doors. It also had striped door trims inside, and a striped sunscreen, also in white and orange, underneath the outer hood.

The three-car range received minor modifications during 1976. A tandem-type master cylinder reservoir protected the contents from leaking completely away, should one side of the casing be punctured, and a tell-tale lamp on the instrument panel warned of low brake fluid level. The split-half sump casing joint was improved with a Loctite sealant and new positioning lugs. Logos on the bootlid returned to a plastic type and the 2CV was given a smaller diameter steering wheel, together with a raised steering ratio. The Spécial only received this modification in April 1977. Identification was easier with a year/model identification plate affixed in the engine bay. New colours stretched the inventiveness of the colour-stylists with such delights as Gazelle Beige, Forget-me-Not Blue and Sun Red for the 2CV4 and 2CV6, though Sun Red was replaced by Geranium Red the same year. A lap-type rear seat belt became available in September 1977.

*July 1990 and a Citroën worker loads some of the last 2CVs on to a West Germany-bound train in Mangualde, Portugal.*

## INTO THE 1980s

The 2CV4 ceased production in September 1978 and the 1979 model range consisted of an improved 2CV Spécial and the 2CV6. The Spécial gained a six-light body, the aluminium trim appeared on the rear doors and wings, and cloth upholstery became an option, together with bucket seats. The centrifugal clutch of the 2CV6 also became a very welcome option. New colours were Nevada Beige, Mimosa Yellow and Mandarine. Brakes were improved with new wheel cylinder fixings in December 1978.

The 1980 model year saw the replacement of the 435cc engine in the 2CV Spécial with the 602cc engine and the model was rechristened the 2CV6 Spécial. Meanwhile, the 2CV6 became the 2CV6 Club. Apart from badging, the 2CV6 Spécial and 2CV6 Club looked much the same. Both received an oil-pressure warning lamp on the instrument panel. New colours appeared for the 1980 season: Azurite Blue and Jade Green.

Another special edition appeared in 1981 – the 2CV6 007 – painted in Mimosa Yellow and released to coincide with the James Bond film *For Your Eyes Only* which appeared that year and which featured a yellow 2CV. Other specials were released too: the 1983 Beachcomber was painted in a suitably maritime blue and white. This car was known in France as the France 3 after the Americas Cup yacht of that name. The Special Bamboo 2CV6 was painted a vivid jungle green. In 1980 another special was to appear, but unlike the others it continued in production and became part of the 2CV range: the Charleston was painted in Burgundy and black and was reminiscent of the Twenties and Thirties Art Deco style. It was so successful that it stayed in the range until the end of production in 1990. Later it was available in yellow and black and in dark and light grey.

*Bare steel bodyshells are finished off at the Mangualde factory in Portugal.*

*Body components are gathered and attached to a jig.*

*The completed body is then dipped into a cleaning bath prior to paint being applied.*

(Above) *Meanwhile, engines are assembled in another part of the factory ...*

(Above right) *... to be fitted to the platform chassis ...*

*... before the body, now painted, is lowered on to the chassis.*

*A body being removed from the etching bath.*

(Below left) *Steering wheels and other components are fitted before the doors.*

(Below) *Completed cars being given final checks.*

Another popular special was the 2CV6 Spécial Dolly, which appeared in 1985. Due to its popularity with women the new 2CV was called the Dolly in a perhaps ill-conceived lapse of political correctness. However, it was extremely popular and was marketed in many combinations of colours. The most popular was perhaps red and white, like the late Dolly in the National Motor Museum, but it also came in grey and white, grey and red, grey and buttermilk, burgundy and buttermilk, green and white, and buttermilk and midnight blue. The Dolly name was stencilled

onto the fresh air flap under the screen in the contrasting colour. The Dolly also sported small stainless hubcaps or embellishers.

The end of the *toute petite voiture* was in sight. While it continued to be popular in export markets including the UK, Belgium and Germany, the 2CV was beginning to slide in France. The last French-built 2CV – a grey 2CV6 Spécial – rolled off the production line at the Levallois factory on 25 February 1988. The factory itself – originally the Clément bicycle factory, but Citroën-owned since 1921 – was outmoded as a

1919 ?

*1990 again and the last few 2CVs from Mangualde are parked in the lot of a French dealer. The end of an era.*

*The last Citroën 2CV, 27 July 1990. A little fanfare, please!*

production factory and it was demolished, without celebration, to sell the valuable city site for property development.

Production was concentrated on the modern factory in Mangualde in Portugal where the last 2CVs were made in the final incarnation of the three-car range: the 2CV6 Spécial with round headlamps, the 2CV6 Club with rectangular headlamps and the popular 2CV6 Charleston with the two-tone paint and chromed round headlamps. All three were powered by the latest 602cc engine first introduced in 1978, but in the new models with an uprated compression ratio of 8.5:1 and some emission control, although the 2CV could never satisfy those regulations completely. The spectre of the new international car production rules on catalytic converters was around the corner and the 2CV could never practically be fitted with such a device. Production continued for two years at Mangualde, where 42,000 further 2CVs were made.

The last 2CV, a grey 2CV6 Charleston, was finished on 27 July 1990 and a tract of motoring history was at an end, after nearly forty-two years of production. The fact that one can't go for many yards down a road without seeing a 2CV or one of its derivatives is due to the huge numbers of them that were built in those years: 5,114,966 2CVs, 1,443,583 Dyanes and nearly 400,000 other variants made up the incredible total of 6,956,895 units.

**French-built 2CV AZL (1969)**

**Engine**

| | |
|---|---|
| Block material | Cast iron |
| Head material | Light alloy |
| Cylinders | Two |
| Cooling | Air |
| Bore and stroke | 66mm × 62mm |
| Capacity | 425cc |
| Valves | OHV |
| Compression ratio | 7.5:1 |
| Carburettor | Solex 28CBI downdraught single barrel |
| Max power | 18bhp at 5,000rpm |
| Max torque | (SAE) 22lbft (3kg m) at 3,000rpm |
| Max engine rpm | 5,200 |
| Lubrication | Gear pump, filter in sump, oil cooler; system capacity 3.87 pints (2.2ltr) |
| Fuel pump | Mechanical |
| Fuel tank capacity | 4.4gal (20ltr) |

**Transmission**

| | |
|---|---|
| Clutch | single dry plate |
| Top gear | 1.473:1 |
| 3rd | 2.137:1 |
| 2nd | 3.571:1 |
| 1st | 7.407:1 |
| Reverse | 8.0:1 |
| Final drive | spiral bevel, axle ratio 3.625:1 |

**Suspension and Steering**

| | |
|---|---|
| Suspension | Independent, front swinging leading arms, two friction dampers, two inertia-type patter dampers; rear independent swinging longitudinal trailing arms linked to front suspension by longitudinal coil springs |
| Shock absorbers | Two inertia-type patter dampers, two telescopic dampers |
| Steering gear | Rack-and-pinion |
| Turning circle between walls | 35ft 1in (10.70m) |
| Turns, lock to lock | 2¼ |
| Tyres | 125 × 380 |

**Brakes**

| | |
|---|---|
| Type | Hydraulic drum |
| Lining area | Front 29.15sq in, rear 30.70sq in |

**Electrical System**

| | |
|---|---|
| Battery | 6-volt, 50Ah |
| Dynamo | 220W |
| Headlamps | Two, height-adjustable from driver's seat |

**French-built 2CV AZL (1969)** (*continued*)

**Dimensions**

| | |
|---|---|
| Track | 4ft 1½in (1,260mm) front and rear |
| Wheelbase | 7ft 10½in (2,400mm) |
| Overall length | 12ft 6in (3,820mm) |
| Overall width | 4ft 10in (1,480mm) |
| Overall height | 5ft 3in (1,600mm) |
| Ground clearance | 6⅓in (160mm) |
| Dry weight | 1,158lb (525kg) |
| Distribution of weight | front 57.1 per cent, rear 42.9 per cent |

**Performance**

| | |
|---|---|
| Max speed in gears | 1st 13mph (21km/h) |
| | 2nd 27.3mph (44km/h) |
| | 3rd 46mph (74km/h) |
| | 4th 59mph (95km/h) |
| Speed in top at 1,000rpm | 12.9mph (20.7km/h) |
| Power-to-weight ratio | 64.4lb/hp (29.2kg/hp) |
| Carrying capacity | 706lb (320kg) |

**Equipment and optional accessories**

Optional centrifugal semi-automatic clutch
Heating by petrol heat exchanger for temperatures below 20°C (68°F)
Separate front seats

| | |
|---|---|
| Price | FF5,655 |

---

**2CV6 (1974)**

**Engine**

| | |
|---|---|
| Construction | All alloy |
| Cylinders | Two |
| Cooling | Air |
| Bore and stroke | 74mm × 70mm |
| Capacity | 602cc |
| Valves | OHV, two per cylinder |
| Compression ratio | 8.5:1 |
| Carburettor | Solex 34 Pics 6 |
| Max power | 28.5bhp at 6,750rpm |
| Max torque | 28.9lbft (3.94kg m) at 3,500rpm |

**2CV6 (1974)** (*continued*)

| | |
|---|---|
| Bearings | Two main |
| Fuel pump | Mechanical |

**Transmission**

| | |
|---|---|
| Type | Four-speed manual |
| Clutch | single dry plate, 6.25in diameter |
| Top gear | 1.32:1 |
| 3rd | 1.79:1 |
| 2nd | 2.66:1 |
| 1st | 5.20:1 |
| Reverse | 5.20:1 |
| Final drive | Spiral bevel |

**Suspension and Steering**

| | |
|---|---|
| Suspension | Front independent by leading arms and horizontal coil springs, interconnected with rear; rear independent by trailing arms and horizontal coil springs, interconnected with front |
| Steering gear | Rack-and-pinion |
| Toe-out | 0.04 to 0.12in |
| Camber | 0 degrees 35 minutes to 1 degree 45 minutes |
| Castor | 15 degrees |
| Rear toe-in | 0 to 0.31 |
| Turning circle between kerbs | 32.5ft (9.9m) |
| Tyres | 125 × 15 Michelin X |
| Pressures | Front 20psi, rear 26psi |
| Wheels | Steel disc three-bolt fixing |

**Brakes**

| | |
|---|---|
| Type | Hydraulic drums, inboard at front, single circuit, manual adjustment |

**Electrical System**

| | |
|---|---|
| Battery | 12-volt, 25Ah |
| Polarity | Negative earth |
| Generator | Alternator |
| Fuses | Four |
| Headlights | Two Cibie halogen |

**Dimensions**

| | |
|---|---|
| Track | 4ft 1½in (1,257mm) front and rear |
| Wheelbase | 7ft 10½in (2,400mm) |
| Overall length | 12ft 6¾in (3,829mm) |
| Overall width | 4ft 10½in (1,486mm) |
| Unladen height | 5ft 3in (1,600mm) |
| Ground clearance | 6½in (165mm) |
| Boot capacity | 7.5 cu ft (0.21 cu m) |

---

**2CV6 (1974)** (*continued*)

**Performance**

| | |
|---|---|
| Maximum speed | 67.1mph (107.9km/h) |
| Fastest | 70.9mph (114.1km/h) |
| Acceleration | 0–30mph 7.2sec |
| | 0–40mph 11.6sec |
| | 0–50mph 18.4sec |
| | 0–60mph 32.8sec |
| Fuel consumption | touring overall 50.9mpg, 5.6ltr × 100km |
| Tank capacity | 4.5gal (20.5ltr) |
| Max range | 229 miles (368km) |

**Equipment**

Breakaway mirror
Energy absorbing steering column
Fresh air ventilation
Hazard warning lights
Outside mirror
Parcel shelf
Sliding roof
Vanity mirror

| | |
|---|---|
| Price | £899 |

---

**2CV6 Special (1982)**

**Engine**

| | |
|---|---|
| Block material | Cast iron |
| Head material | Aluminium alloy |
| Cylinders | Two |
| Cooling | Air |
| Bore and stroke | 74mm × 70mm |
| Capacity | 602cc |
| Valves | OHV |
| Cam drive | Pinion |
| Compression ratio | 8.5:1 |
| Carburettor | Twin-choke Solex |
| Bearings | Two main |
| Max power | 29bhp (DIN) at 5,750rpm |
| Max torque | 29lbft (3.96kg m) at 3,500rpm |
| Fuel capacity | 5.5gal (25ltr) |

**2CV6 Special (1982)** (*continued*)

**Transmission**

| | |
|---|---|
| Gearbox | Four-speed manual |
| Clutch | 6.25in single dry plate, actuated by cable |
| Top gear | 1.32:1 |
| 3rd | 1.79:1 |
| 2nd | 2.66:1 |
| 1st | 5.20:1 |
| Reverse | 5.20:1 |
| Final drive | 4.125:1 |

**Suspension and Steering**

| | |
|---|---|
| Front with rear | Independent by leading arms and horizontal coil springs, interconnected |
| Rear with front | Independent by trailing arms and horizontal coil springs, interconnected |
| Steering gear | Rack-and-pinion |
| Tyres | Michelin 125 × 15 |
| Pressures | Front 20psi, rear 26psi |
| Wheels | Pressed steel 4j × 15 |

**Brakes**

| | |
|---|---|
| Front | Discs, 9.6in diameter |
| Rear | Drums, 7.1in diameter |

**Performance**

| | |
|---|---|
| Maximum speed | 67mph (107km/h) |
| Fastest | 71.1mph (114.4km/h) |
| Acceleration | 0–30mph 6.8sec |
| | 0–40mph 11.3sec |
| | 0–50mph 18.4sec |
| | 0–60mph 32.1sec |
| | Standing ¼ mile (0.4km) 23.6sec |
| Fuel consumption | Touring 50.2mpg (5.63ltr × 100km) |
| | Overall 38.8mpg (7.28ltr × 100km) |
| Max range | 276 miles (444km) |
| Weight | |
| Unladen | 11.6cwt (587kg) |
| As tested | 15.3cwt (777kg) |
| | |
| Price | £1,834 (£2,284.85 including VAT) |

**2CV6 Charleston (1985)**

**Engine**

| | |
|---|---|
| Cylinders | Two |
| Cooling | Air |
| Bore and stroke | 74mm × 70mm |
| Capacity | 602cc |
| Valves | OHV |
| Compression ratio | 8.5:1 |
| Carburettor | Solex twin choke |
| Max power | 29bhp at 5,750rpm |
| Max torque | 29lbft (3.96kg m) at 3,500rpm |
| Fuel capacity | 6.6 US gal (25ltr) |

**Transmission**

| | |
|---|---|
| Gearbox | Four-speed manual |
| Top gear | 5.45:1 |
| 3rd | 7.39:1 |
| 2nd | 10.99:1 |
| 1st | 21.48:1 |
| Final drive | 4.13:1 |
| Speeds in gears | Top (5,650rpm) 71mph (114km/h) |
| | 3rd (6,750rpm) 62mph (100km/h) |
| | 2nd (6,750rpm) 42mph (68km/h) |
| | 1st (6,750rpm) 22mph (35km/h) |

**Suspension and Steering**

| | |
|---|---|
| Front | Leading arms, coil springs interconnected with the rear, horizontal tube shock absorbers |
| Rear | Trailing arms, coil springs interconnected with the front, horizontal tube shock absorbers |
| Steering gear | Rack-and-pinion |
| Turns, lock to lock | Three |
| Turning circle | 36ft 8½in (11.20m) |
| Tyres | Michelin X 125R × 15 |
| Wheels | Steel disc 15 × 4J |

**Brakes**

| | |
|---|---|
| Front | 9.5in inboard discs |
| Rear | 7.1 × 1.3in drums |
| Swept area | 249sq in |
| Minimum stopping distance | 154ft at 60mph (46.9m at 97km/h) |
| Pedal effort for 0.5g stop | 25lb (11.3kg) |
| Fade | 28 per cent increase in pedal effort to maintain 0.5g deceleration in six stops from 50mph (80km/h) |

**2CV6 Charleston (1985)** (*continued*)

**Instrumentation**

| | |
|---|---|
| Gauges | 130km/h speedometer |
| | 99,999 odometer |
| | Fuel level |
| | Voltmeter |
| Warning lights | Oil pressure |
| | Alternator |
| | Headlights on |
| | High beam |
| | Hazard |
| | Indicators |

**Dimensions**

| | |
|---|---|
| Track | 4ft 1⅓in (1,260mm) front and rear |
| Wheelbase | 7ft 10⅓in (2,400mm) |
| Overall length | 12ft 7in (3,830mm) |
| Overall width | 4ft 10in (1,480mm) |
| Overall height | 5ft 3in (1,600mm) |
| Ground clearance | 7½in (191mm) |
| Overhang front/rear | 26½/29¾in (673/757mm) |
| Boot space | 8.9/44cu ft (252/1246cu cm); second figure denotes with rear seat removed |
| Test weight | 1,440lb (654kg) |
| Weight distribution | 57/43 per cent |

**Performance**

| | |
|---|---|
| Maximum speed | 71mph (114km/h) |
| Acceleration | 0–30mph 5.7sec |
| | 0–50mph 16.9sec |
| | 0–60mph 27.3sec |
| Fuel consumption | Normal driving 42.5mpg (US gallons) (5.53ltr × 100km) |
| Range | 190 miles (305km) |
| Interior noise | Idle in neutral dBA 56 |
| | Maximum 1st gear dBA 85 |
| | Constant 30mph dBA 69 |
| | 50mph dBA 81 |

**Maintenance**

| | |
|---|---|
| Oil/filter change | 5,000 miles |
| Chassis lubrication | 5,000 miles |
| Tune-up | 10,000 miles |
| | |
| Price | US $6,495 |

## Prices of the 2CV for the first ten years of production

*Four-door Berline*

1950 France (October 1950, inc. tax)
FF283,000
1951 France (October 1951, inc. tax)
FF289,000
1952 France (October 1952, inc. tax)
FF340,950
1953 France (March 1953, inc. tax)
FF341,870
England (October 1953, inc. PT)
£565
1954 France (December 1954, inc. tax)
FF341,870
England (January 1954, inc. PT)
£565
1955 France (August 1955, ex. tax)
A model          FF346,200
AZ model         FF362,400
1956 France (October 1956, ex. tax)
A model          FF352,100
AZ model         FF373,600
England (January 1956, inc. PT)
AZ model         £598
USA (East Coast POE price)
AZ/AZL models    $1,145/1,250
1957 France (October 1957, ex. tax)
A model          FF374,000
AZ model         FF403,500
AZL model        FF424,000
AZLM model       FF430,000
England (January 1957, inc. PT)
AZ model         £598
USA (East Coast POE price)
AZ/AZL models    $1,295/1,395
1958 France (October 1958, ex. tax)
AZ model         FF389,400
AZL model        FF420,400
AZLM model       FF447,600
England (January 1958 inc. PT)
AZ model         £598
USA (East Coast POE price)
AZL model        $1,295

1959 France (October 1959 ex. tax)
AZL model        FF467,125
AZLM model       FF473,625
AZ model         FF444,925
4×4 model Sahara FF862,010
England (April 1959 inc. PT)
AZ model         £565
(October 1959 inc. PT)
BJ model Bijou   £674
USA (East Coast POE price)
AZL model        $1,300
1960 France (October 1960 ex. tax)
AZ model         NF4,725
AZL model        NF4,790
AZLM model       NF5,031
4×4 model Sahara NF8,706
England (December 1960 inc. PT)
BJ model Bijou   £695

*Light Van AZU Model 1954–60*

1954 France (March 1954, ex. tax) FF346,950
     England (December 1954)    £478
1955 France (August 1955)       FF368,000
     England (January 1955)     £478
1956 England (September 1956)   £489
1957 France (October 1957)      FF425,000
     England (January 1957)     £489
1958 France (October 1958)      FF449,700
     England (January 1958)     £489
1959 France (October 1959)      FF470,495
     England (April 1959)       £415
1960 France (October 1960)      NF4,815
     England (January 1960)     £415

*Pickup AZP Model 1954–59 (Slough-Built Only)*

1954 England (December 1954)    £478
1955 England (January 1955)     £478
1956 England (January 1956)     £491
1957 England (January 1957)     £489
1958 England (January 1958)     £489
1959 England (April 1959)       £415

## Chassis start numbers

The following list gives the first chassis number of a year batch in all model variants of the standard 2CV.

1949 2CV A – 1
1950 2CV A – 924
1951 2CV A – 7100
    2CV AU – 300000
1952 2CV A – 21850
    2CV AU – 301700
1953 2CV A – 43153
    2CV AU – 309450
1954 2CV A – 77250
    2CV AU – 322500
1955 2CV A – 121200
    2CV AZ – 156750
    2CV AU – 346950
    2CV AZU – 368000
1956 2CV A – 125101
    2CV AZ – 229501
    2CV AZU – 368000
1957 2CV A – 125315
    2CV AZ – 321315
    2CV AZL – 321315
    2CV AZU – 950729
1958 2CV A – 125372
    2CV AZL – 424015
    2CV AZU – 530595
1959 2CV A – 125478
    2CV AZL – 1061832
    2CV AZU – 1061831
1960 2CV A – 125564
    2CV AZL – 1134100
    2CV AZU – 606601
1961 2CV AZL – 2396500
1962 2CV AZL – 2591864
1963 2CV AZL – 8297629
    2CV AZAM – 8297629
1964 2CV AZ – 8561201
    2CV AZAM – 1435001
1965 2CV AZL – 1643042
    2CV AZAM – 1700036
1966 2CV AZL – 1840000
    2CV AZAM – 1865000
    2CV AZU – 1185001

1967 2CV AZL – 7028000
    2CV AZAM – 7055000
1968 2CV AZL – 7177000
1969 2CV AZA – 7197000
    2CV AZU – 7125700
1970 2CV AZL – 7235001
    2CV4 – 7850001
    2CV6 – 00KA001
    2CV AZU – 7137201
1971 2CV4 – 7888001
    2CV6 – 00KA4001
1972 2CV4 – 7960001
    2CV6 – 05KA20001
    2CV AZU – 7156501
1973 2CV4 – 9016001
    2CV6 – 10KA5001
    2CV AZU – 7815001
1974 2CV4 – 09066001
    2CV6 – 15KA6501
1975 2CV4 – 09140001
    2CV6 – 23KA8001
1976 2CV4 – 00KB0001
    2CV6 – 30KA9001
1977 2CV4 – 06KB0001
    2CV6 – 38KA0001
1978 2CV6 – 44KA5001
1979 2CV6 – 50KA5001
1980 2CV6 – 56KA4001
1981 2CV6 – 68KA0001
1982 2CV6 – 77KA5001
1983 2CV6 – 88KA2001
1984 2CV6 – 96KA6001
1985 2CV6 – KA038501
1986 2CV6 Special, Charleston – KA110001
1987 2CV6 all models – KA192501

The last model produced in France was No 00KA302493, on 25 February 1988. The last model produced in Portugal was No 00KA376002, on 27 July 1990. The last right-hand drive 2CV made in Portugal – a red and white Dolly – is in the National Motor Museum at Beaulieu.

# 5  Derivatives

## AMI

The Ami derivative of the 2CV made its debut in 1961. Its main purpose was to fill the gap in the Citroën range between the cheap 2CV and the big and complex two-litre ID/DS saloons. Development and construction costs were kept to a minimum by basing the new vehicle on the tried-and-tested chassis and mechanical components of the 2CV.

From a mechanical point of view the Ami-6, as the first variant was known, differed from the 2CV mainly in the size of its engine. Still the familiar horizontally-opposed, twin-cylinder, air-cooled unit, it was overbored to 74mm to give a swept volume of 602cc, making it a fiscal 3CV. In original form, the engine put out 22bhp as compared to the 13bhp of the contemporary 425cc 2CV, but power was increased to 25 bhp in 1963 and to 35bhp in 1965, for the final years of production.

Although the Ami was designed to occupy a higher step in the Citroën hierarchy, it managed to be considerably quirkier than, and lack the charm of, the original little car.

*An Ami pushed hard like this displays extreme body roll. However, with the radial tyres and soft suspension they are very difficult to unstick.*

*Rennes-la-Janais in Brittany where early Ami models are under construction in 1962, when 600 were produced daily.*

Slab-sided styling was to be expected, as were lights faired into the body-pressings, but what spoilt the design for many critics was the reverse-rake rear window. This design was supposed to cut down reflections and keep rain water off the rear screen, but only two other European cars (the Ford Anglia and the Consul Classic) adopted it and it rapidly became apparent that the vast majority of the public were not impressed with the gimmick. However, this treatment places any of the three vehicles in an immediately recognizable and precise time-frame. Equipment levels of the Ami were rather higher than those of the 2CV, and there was a 'proper' boot as well. Interior details mirrored the ID/DS with the single-spoke steering wheel, and door handles. It sold very well on the home market, probably on the strength of its combination of cheapness and respectable performance and comfort levels – in fact, the French

bought every one the factory at Rennes-la-Janais could make. Sales had gone ahead of the 2CV by 1965 and for many years the Ami-6 was France's top-selling car. By the end of production in 1969 851,220 of all Ami types had been built. In Britain it was a different story: it did not go on sale until October 1966, in Saloon Tourisme, Saloon Confort and Estate versions, and sadly it went down like a lead balloon.

(Above) *Interior of a 1966 Ami-6 shows the fairly 'snazzy' styling with door trims and the single-spoke steering wheel borrowed from the DS model.*

*An Ami-6 definitely at home. The Ami would outsell the 2CV during its production run: to some it is ugly, but not – quite obviously – to all those buyers.*

The Ami-6 saloon was joined in 1964 by an Estate version, or 'break' as the French called it, deriving the word with no feeling for Anglo-Saxon spelling from the English term 'shooting brake'. Although still curious to look at, this was nothing like the aesthetic disaster of the saloon, with which it shared all exterior dimensions and mechanical details. The Ami-6 Saloon and Estate Confort got sliding front windows in October 1967. The Estate continued in production a few months longer than the saloon version, overlapping during 1969 with the new Ami-8, which was introduced at that year's Geneva Show.

The Ami-8 tried to put right all the aesthetic wrongs of the Ami-6 in an attempt to broaden its potential market. Although its general outline was similar to that of the superseded model, there were several differences: the reverse-rake rear window disappeared in favour of a sportier semi-fastback style; door handles were now recessed; and there were quarter-lights at the front in place of the original model's sliding windows. The pressed 'ribs' behind the front wheel arch were gone, and the large scuttle air intake was diminished to blend in better with the overall styling. The new bumpers looked less like an afterthought, and there were stylish rectangular side/indicator lights in place of the earlier car's simple round units. Headlights were sunk into styled recesses, and a rubbing strip at the base of the side indentation helped to make the appearance less top-heavy, as well as providing some protection to the doors against accidental damage. Ami-6 estates continued to be available alongside the Ami-8 saloons until they, too, were replaced, by an estate version of the Ami-8, in the autumn of 1969. This shared all the styling improvements of the saloon, except for its retention of sliding windows at the front.

*A spare wheel is strapped into the spacious engine bay of the Ami.*

In mechanical specification, these 8s were identical to the earlier 6s, though the drum brakes of the first 8s were replaced by discs in autumn 1969 and the Estate version always had discs. Power output remained at the 35bhp of the last Ami-6s until production ended in 1978. In the meantime, however, a re-engined version intended to appeal higher up the market had appeared. This was the Ami Super, introduced in April 1973 for both home and UK markets, with the 1015cc air-cooled flat-four power unit first seen in the 1970 GS models. This produced 55.5bhp, 5.5bhp less than in GS form, and drove through a four-speed all-synchromesh gearbox with floor-mounted selector lever to give the car a maximum speed of 87mph. New suspension featured anti-roll bars at front and rear, and there were more powerful disc brakes from the 1972 GS 1220 model. Both saloon and estate versions were available, and survived in production alongside the Ami-8s until all four models were replaced by the Visa in 1978.

(Above) *Ami-6 suspension showing the horizontally mounted telescopic shock absorber.*

*Club models of the Ami-6 were distinguished by the twin headlamps and upgraded specifications.*

*The Ami-6 van has a
distinctly hearse-like
appearance ...*

*... while the estate is a good-
looking and usable load
carrier.*

*This late-1964 Ami-6 is in fine standard condition. The Ami models outsold the 2CV for many years.*

*The controversial reverse-raked rear screen of the Ami-6 apparently kept the rain off the glass.*

*Definitely a cute car, the early Ami-6 has quite a cult following and you can see why!*

There were minor changes over the years. From September 1970, a model known as the Ami-8 Confort was available with certain sophistications like winding instead of sliding windows. It was distinguished by the Citroën chevrons on its grille. The Club model introduced at the same time had stainless steel window surrounds and side stripes. From October 1973 the 8 Saloon Luxe was redesignated Confort, and the Confort model name disappeared the following October. From January 1975, both 8 and Super models were fitted with a hazard warning light system as standard, and jersey upholstery was specified. The 8s had bench front seats, while the Supers had reclining front bucket seats. These recliners became available on the 8s in September 1975, when a folding rear seat was added to the specification of

*Ami interiors were much more luxurious than those of the 2CV. The steering wheel is from the DS/ID models and the instrumentation is much more comprehensive. Trim and upholstery levels are much smarter, too.*

*The otherwise spacious engine bay is filled with the spare wheel.*

*Later restyling exercises on the Ami range lost the early model's distinct charm. This 1964 example belongs to Ray Stark.*

both 8 and Super estates. At the same time, a heated rear window was made standard on all Super models. A new colour range for the 8s arrived in November 1976, bringing with it colour-keyed and revised interior trim, and 8 production stopped in February 1978.

It is perhaps odd to consider in retrospect that the most popular models for the collector today are the early Ami-6 models with reverse-rake rear window and ugly-duckling styling. In fact, the Ami-8 is now considered the ugly one! It is true that the Ami-8 had a smoother line and less idiosyncratic character, but in these days of motor cars designed by computer and all looking the same, the appearance of an early Ami-6, with all its odd bits of design and quirky styling, is like a breath of fresh air.

*(Above) More lifestyle advertising, and with the rear seat folded flat you probably could fit four Great Danes in the back of a 1969 Ami-8.*

*(Below) Frontal treatment was tidied up for the Ami-8, but purists prefer the quirkier early Ami-6 shape, ugly or not.*

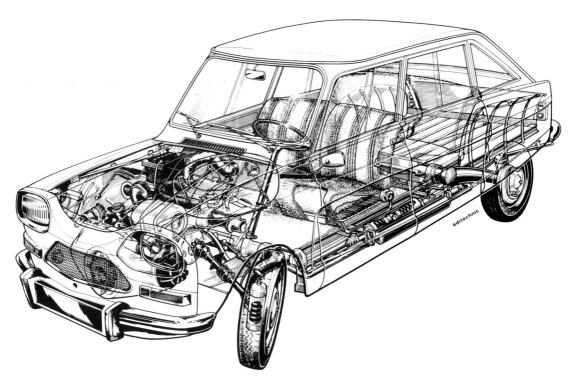

*1969 Ami-8 cutaway showing suspension units with, on the nearest side, the exhaust silencer right alongside.*

*The Ami Super was similar to the 8, but with a grille lightened by the horizontal bar incorporating the Citroën symbol.*

# DYANE

The Dyane appeared at the 1967 Paris Motor Show and immediately suspicions were raised that it was to be a long-term 2CV replacement, particularly as it shared that car's mechanical specification, but with a rather more consciously styled and better-equipped body. Citroën itself was saying nothing, however, protecting its options, and in due course the Dyane settled comfortably into a niche as a complementary model to the 2CV. The difference has been aptly summed up in the description of the Dyane as being a 'city' car while the 2CV is a 'country' car.

The first Dyanes had 21bhp from the 425cc engine which differed only in detail from that in the contemporary 2CVs. They were rated as a fiscal 2CV and were capable of around 56mph. In March 1968 came a slightly enlarged engine of 435cc, giving 26bhp at 6,750rpm and a top speed of 64mph. This was the Dyane-4, which was to be joined in September 1968 by the Dyane-6 model with the 602cc Ami engine, a fiscal 3CV. As fitted to the Dyanes, the 602cc unit initially developed 28bhp, rather less than in its Ami form, but it was soon uprated to give 33bhp, and by 1972 to give 35bhp. The Dyane-4 arrived in Britain in 1970 and was withdrawn in January 1974, leaving only the Dyane-6 model in production.

*Early Dyanes had this mesh-type grille. Designed as a replacement for the 2CV – a fact Citroën may have disputed – the Dyane found its own market niche.*

The idea of the Dyane body was to uprate the specifications and appearance while retaining the basic theme of the 2CV. It had larger glass area, in particular the windscreen, squarer and less obviously 'vintage' front wings – although separate front wings were themselves an oddity by 1967 – and headlamps recessed into these wings instead of perched on top. The body itself was a little wider, although overall dimensions remained similar and luggage access was improved by a hinged rear panel, estate fashion, instead of the 2CV's bootlid. There were plastic push-button door handles, and of course a wider plastic grille to go with the wider bonnet. The first bodies were of a four-light design with thick rear pillars, but later a six-light design was introduced, the extra windows being similar to the 2CV's. Instrumentation was more comprehensive than in the 2CV, and the inner door panels were moulded to give side armrests. Sliding front windows were fitted, Ami-fashion, instead of the 2CV's hinged panes.

Three special Dyane variants were made before the model disappeared, first with the Dyane-4 in 1975 and then the Dyane-6 in 1984. The specials were the Capra, Caban and the Cote d'Azur, the latter being painted white with blue striping. More than 1,400,000 Dyanes of all types had been built.

There is no doubt that the Dyane is as rugged and practical as the original 2CV and quite as cheap to own – although slightly more expensive to buy – and nowadays nearly as popular. But it is unlikely ever to have the following of the good old 2CV. It was a good attempt by Citroën to bring the 2CV up to date, but they didn't figure on the original 2CV having such a following.

*Early Dyanes were four-light but this 1971 example has the familiar six-light body. The Dyane was the first true hatchback, although the idea had been explored with the 2CV Commerciale.*

*A Dyane 6 showing the odd door handles and large rear hatch door.*

(Below) *Later Dyanes had this grey plastic grille. Note the air intake under the screen.*

*This 1980 model has a black grille and detail changes like the indicator repeaters on the front wings.*

## MEHARI

The multi-role Méhari was designed with several uses in mind to maximize its market appeal. Forestry and agriculture presented a niche, as did safari trips and even airport use. Of course the most fashionable use was as the beach buggy type of fun car, reminiscent of the Mini Moke.

Based on a strengthened Dyane platform chassis capable of carrying a 400kg payload, the chassis is also plated underneath to protect it from the elements. The engine is the 602cc unit and the transmission is given special gearbox ratios. The layout is essentially a pickup with tiny doors which could be specified to be replaced by simple chains run across the door openings. The important difference between this and other beach buggy types was the all-plastic non-corroding body made by the heatform specialists SEAB in France as eleven flexible panels screwed or riveted on to a steel frame. The result is a durable, light yet tough body without the need for the manufacturers to apply body colour, as the plastic is self-coloured. The plastic, known as Cycolac ABS (*Acrylonitrile Butadiene Styrene*) starts out as a by-product of the coal and petroleum industries. In a process developed by Marbon in Amsterdam and also in Grangemouth, the plastic is made by reducing the raw ingredients to a powder which is heated, mixed and formed into rods. These are then granulated, colouring agent is added and then the material is amalgamated by heating and rolled into flat sheets for delivery to the heatform factory where the body components are made.

(Above) *The Méhari is launched to the press on 16 May 1968 at Deauville golf course on the Channel coast where, I imagine, there would be little big game to hunt!*

*Méhari meeting in Hagan, Germany, in June 1992.*

The Méhari was launched in May 1968, initially as a two-seater. However, the market quickly demanded four seats, which became available in 1969. Disc brakes appeared in 1978 and the dashboard was revised in 1980 to include round instruments. A natural progression for a vehicle of this type was to develop a four-wheel drive version and from 1979 the 4×4 was made available, with three of the four forward gears given a reducing gear to provide seven forward ratios and a differential lock. Unlike the

2CV Sahara (*see* below), there was only one engine in the Méhari, but it was uprated over the years to provide more power, and roughly followed the Dyane's progress in that areas. The new 4×4 versions had a new grille and a bonnet-mounted spare wheel. Proving popular, the grille became available on the two-wheel drive versions from 1983. The 4×4 was only made in limited numbers, however, with only 1,313 being made in the three years to 1982. Five thousand 4×4 Méharis were ordered by the French army in 1981, but these models were to be fitted with steel bodies and have the 652cc LNA/Visa engines.

(Above) *The Belgian-built Méhari dashboard showing the textured grip flooring. The Méhari model is not a standard fitting!*

*A 4×4 Méhari climbs an almost impossible slope in July 1979 as a passenger in the rear holds on tight. The name Méhari comes from the favoured type of* Dromedary *for rapid, long-distance desert travel – the car was made on a Dyane chassis, but the body was all plastic, mounted on a steel frame.*

*A 1989 2CV6 Special Dolly in typical pose, at home in the city or on the village green.*

*Side view shows successful use of two-tone colour scheme.*

*With the grille muff – a standard item of 2CV equipment ...*

*... And without.*

(Above) *Extra trim on the doors brightens the appearance.*

(Right) *The latest version of the 2CV sported square rear lamps and a heavy bumper.*

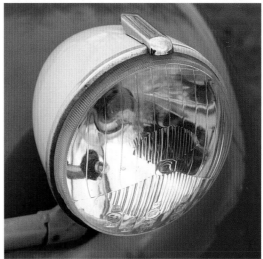

(Above left) *Stainless surround on the front window countered corrosion.*

(Above) *Round headlamps proved more popular than rectangular ones.*

(Left) *The beech 'scotch' in use prevented the car falling off the jack when changing a wheel.*

(Above) *4×4 Méhari with hard top. Between 1979 and 1983 1,213 were built.*

*1982 Méhari engine bay. Note the car jack mounted on the left side. The spare wheel was mounted upright behind the front seat.*

This handmade 2CV model from Columbia is particularly charming.

(Right) This 1963 AZU van is owned by Graham Draper, whose Sussex-based restoration company, Garage Levallois, offers completely rebuilt 2CVs for sale.

(Below) This 1961 AZL – L for Luxe – sported trim on the bonnet and below the doors, alloy spats and a two-horse mascot made by Robri.

(Below right) A very tidy 2CV engine bay showing heater trunking, very clean exhaust manifolds and the exposed teeth of the flywheel with the top-mounted starter motor.

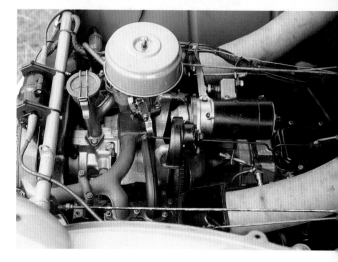

(Above) *Totally rebuilt 2CVs like this one are available from Garage Levallois. The chassis has been replaced and usually new interior trim, running gear and engine are fitted.*

(Below left) *The late engine bay sports more plastic, such as on the air cleaner and alternator electrics.*

(Below right) *The simple interior of a newly rebuilt 2CV will give years of service.*

*This 1990 2CV Dolly was one of the last built and is in the National Motor Museum. It has only delivery mileage on the clock*

*The 2CV is immediately identifiable by children because it sports a recognizable and happy face. This model is a one-off.*

*This 1985 2CV Charleston proved a popular type with several two-tone paint combinations available. Photographed in northern Italy by Maurice Rowe.*

*Méhari 4×4 showing the difference between the 2CV and 4×4 chassis.*

The Méhari was in production for a total of nineteen years to 1987 and 144,953 were built, all for the French market. They found their way into several public service uses as lightweight go-anywhere vehicles with tough scratchproof bodies and the tried-and-tested air-cooled engines. The model was certainly a good 'experiment' to test the viability of all-plastic bodies which could be made and assembled quickly, unlike the GRP bodies of other cars which have to be layered in a smelly and time-consuming job lasting perhaps days. The exercise proved that it was possible, but the plastic itself was expensive to buy and repair.

## THE SAHARA

This press release was published in 1954, and by the sound of it the Sahara was designed for a bigger audience than it got in the end. The following text was originally in French, translated to English:

### THE CITROËN 2CV 4×4 SAHARA

Aware of the problems of oil prospecting in the Sahara, the Citroën company has perfected a 2HP model with four-wheel drive, thus adding to the car's already well-known qualities (light weight, economy, sturdiness, low maintenance cost, air-cooling, etc.) and incredible manoeuvrability over sand.

The 2HP '4×4', fully loaded, can go up a 45% grade, and do it over sand (45% represents three times the slope over the road over Izoard Pass, one of the steepest highways in France).

'He who does more can also do less'. First designed for the Sahara, this true mechanical workhorse will prove of tremendous use wherever road conditions are such as to prevent normal automotive traffic. (The car has its contribution to make to large-scale farming and ranching, public works projects, the construction of funicular railways, or of dams; it is cut out for work as liaison vehicle in underdeveloped territories, etc.) The 4×4 2HP is, in fact, particularly well suited for travel over sand or other loose, unstable terrains, thanks to the following characteristics: low net weight (about 1,400lb); nearly equal distribution of weight over each wheel; four independently sprung wheels linked by an interacting suspension system running

*The 2CV 4×4, or 'Sahara', appeared in 1958 and deserved to do better than it did. The basic idea involved fitting an engine at front and rear, each driving its own set of wheels.*

longitudinally on each side between front and rear wheelbase; outsize tyres under very low pressure; a relatively high-powered engine system (about 28 French HP).

**Technical Details**

Front and rear axles are powered by two quite independent engine assemblies (each with its own motor and transmission). There are two air-cooled horizontal bi-cylindrical [sic] engines, each with a capacity of 425cc and each producing about 14 French HP. The transmissions furnish four speeds, as on a normal 2HP. There is no special device to ensure synchronization of the two engines. On the contrary, front and rear wheels can, when necessary, revolve at different speeds, thus affording increased manoeuvrability over terrains presenting different surface conditions beneath each wheelbase. When surface conditions are identical (as on the highway or over a packed earth trail), the two engines fall naturally into synchronization with each other. The normal 2HP carburettors have been especially modified to prevent coughing or choking on steep climbs. Linked by cable, they are thus simultaneously commanded by the accelerator pedal. The two clutches

are also commanded by a single pedal (again through cable linkage). The two transmissions are commanded simultaneously by a single shift lever. By means of a special disjunctor, the rear transmission may be shifted to neutral without affecting command over the forward transmission. In this way, the car can proceed on the front engine only; there is thus provision for economizing petrol consumption over easy surfaces. It has a $8 \times 31$ conical coupling (final drive). Reinforced overseas type chassis with the underside of both engines protected by skis, a system which allows deep ruts to be crossed without danger to the car. Tubular front and rear bumpers (at both front and rear, the vehicle can be lifted and released by hand from mud or any other obstacle).

Since the rear of this car is likely to bear more weight than the normal 2HP, the frame has been built to lie in a completely horizontal plane, so that the whole portion of the chassis lying ahead of the forward axle is raised, the car acquiring greater manoeuvrability over rough terrain. The brakes, located at the working ends of forward and rear transmissions, have been well protected against the intrusion of mud or dust. The car utilizes X-type tyres, most

*This sort of terrain is no problem for the 4×4, which is easily recognizable by the spare wheel strapped to the bonnet.*

(Below) *A Sahara makes it to the top of a steep hill during tests.*

suitable for driving over sand, thanks to treads that cannot lose their shape. These tyres are, moreover, very oversized. The 155 × 400 X-type tyre is capable of supporting 1,750lb per axle, whereas the load weight per axle on the 2HP 4×4 Sahara does not overstep a maximum of 1,034lb (704lb empty). Tyre pressure can, without risk, be reduced to 91/2psi, a great advantage over bad surfaces. The same pressure can be maintained while travelling, so that continual bleeding and refilling of tyres is avoided. The spare tyre is located on the bonnet.

Performance: With its full load (four adults) the car can be driven over any sort of surface and can climb up slopes of about 45%.

Speed over the highway: more than 60mph.

Petrol consumption: 31mpg on the highway; 23–25 mpg over other surfaces.

Another release gave examples of situations in which the 4×4 was deemed the ideal workhorse:

> ... It is especially well suited to:

- Public Service work. It goes everywhere and suits the needs of the foreman of dam, pipe-line and funicular construction work.
- To electric, water and gas distributors when supervision and maintenance of electric cables or different pipe-lines in the wilderness is needed. – To topographers and geologists. It allows a team of two men to carry 150kg of material, to reach their working spot whatever the ground may be like.
- To large scale farming. The 2HP 4×4 replaces slow and heavy tractors advantageously for all light work such as the destruction of insects in orchards.
- To forest rangers. As a means of rapid transportation, it enables them to get through the most difficult and steepest forest paths to stop and locate forest fires.
- To milk-collectors or to isolated farmers in mountain areas who are very difficult to reach in winter time.
- To country doctors, veterinarians and artificial inseminators who are called day and night, in all seasons and in any kind of weather.

To these customers, the 4×4 2HP adds to its driving possibilities and to its manoeuvrability, the comfort of a waterproof and warm body-work:
- To some public services such as the French Telephone and Telegraph Company and the French Police which must assure mail distribution or inspection and sometimes, help in the most difficult areas in all seasons.

- To agricultural, mining and industrial activities located in overseas territories as a liaison car, able to travel through the bush and where no roads exist.

## FOURGONNETTE VAN

In 1951, after two years of 2CV production, Citroën launched the Fourgonnette AU van. This had the same chassis as the 2CV, but the body was taller, wider and quite a bit shorter. From the rear edge of the front doors the 2CV bodywork was replaced by a boxy corrugated steel body with double doors at the rear, each sporting an elongated 'porthole' window. The doors had extending checkstraps at each side. The model shared the 2CV's 20ltr fuel tank, but this was moved from between the chassis to the right side of the van with a filler tube and cap set into a niche in the corrugated side section, and the spare wheel was fitted to the left, accessible through a hatch in the corrugated bodywork in front of the rear wheel. Michelin *Pilote* 135 × 400 section tyres were fitted in place of the 125 section. The front wing was fitted with a very necessary rear-view mirror. Payload was calculated at 250kg with a 1.8cu m load space. Top speed was around 60km/h. In September 1952 head gaskets were omitted, as on the saloons; in October that year, exterior colours were a darker grey with yellow wheels and in June 1953 the engine fan was made with four blades. September 1954 saw the arrival of the AZ range in Saloon (AZ) and Fourgonnette (AZU) forms with the new 425cc engine. The van did not get a centrifugal clutch, but received an independent stop light at the rear where the tail light was fitted to the other side of the number plate.

Sometime around 1956 the method of attaching the corrugated roof to the front bulkhead behind the driving cabin was changed. Earlier models had a simple, spot-welded flange folding from the roof panel down onto the bulkhead and exposed both to the weather and to view. Later types had a neater but more complicated joint formed by extending the leading edge forward and hiding the spot-welded join under the slight overhang. Altogether a neater, more professional-looking job.

Apart from the addition of a defroster in November 1957, nothing changed until the appearance of a new bonnet and grille in July 1961, with the original wing mirror still in place. The bonnet was much tidier in appearance with a smaller, lower grille. Later that year the colour range was extended to either a grey exterior with green interior or pastel yellow exterior with red interior. February 1962 saw the van sharing the same uprated engine of the Saloon, producing 13.5bhp at 4,000rpm. The next year saw changes to the van body, including flat sections above the centreline to permit signwriting on the van sides. The rear windows were squared off with rounded corners and a new window was added at the forward end of the van to improve the light inside. A reinforced bumper was also fitted, and front brakes were improved by

the addition of wheel cylinders from the Ami-6. Engines were uprated to 18bhp, but with a Zenith 28 IN carburettor instead of the Solex 28CB1.

The AK350 model, the designation of which denoted an increase in payload to 350kg, appeared in April 1963 with the Ami-6 engine of 602cc giving 22bhp at 4,500rpm, and the Ami-6 gearbox. Load space went up to 2.1cu m and the 350 had $135 \times 380$ tyres like the saloons since September 1959. The next year the AZU got tubeless 125 section tyres. Colours were exactly the same as for the AZU model, which continued unaltered in production.

In February 1966 the AK350 got 12-volt electrics with a belt-driven alternator in place of the dynamo, and a month later the double transmission joints were replaced by 'homokinetic', or constant velocity, joints. Power was increased on the AZU in August 1967 to 21bhp with a 7.75 compression ratio and the Solex 32 PICS carburettor. This increased top speed to 80km/h and gave petrol consumption of 6.5ltr $\times$ 100km. An entirely new gearbox was fitted to the AK350 in October 1967, but retaining the earlier gear ratios. The clutch cable was re-routed and the gearbox oil capacity changed to 0.9ltr, of 80 E.P.

*A Fourgonnette from around 1954. The hatch behind the door houses the spare wheel. An extended-arm rear view mirror was standard equipment.*

December 1967 saw replacement of the steel camshaft of the AZU engine with a cast version, and new pushrods and rocker shafts. Early next year the gearbox ratios were changed and two months later the engine of the AK350 was changed to the 602cc type with an 8.5:1 compression ratio, providing 33bhp. New gear ratios appeared and the brake pedal was changed to a pendant type. In April 1969, Armco brake pipes were fitted to the AK and in July the suspension pots on AZU models were modified.

In July 1970 a new Fourgonnette arrived as the AKS400, mechanically similar to the AK350 but with a taller rear van cab and correspondingly bigger rear door windows, and with fewer but wider ribs on the lower panels. Payload went up to 475kg and the AKS400 had a top speed of 85km/h and fuel consumption of 7–8ltr × 100km.

The name changed again in October 1971 to the AZU250 and a revised specification was published in 1972 giving the power as 21bhp at 5,250rpm; a new gearbox and

*An early AZU Fourgonnette with the exposed welded joint between the body bulkhead and the roof which ...*

*... was improved in the later models by concealing the welded joint under a lip where it was less prone to unsightly corrosion.*

*By 1965 the AK Fourgonnette had addressed the problem of the dark payload space with the added window. Later, a fluted bonnet appeared in line with the saloon cars.*

*All Fourgonnettes had the exterior rear door check straps to hold the doors in the open position. The divided number plate with central plate lamp is a standard 2CV fitting.*

ratios; minor changes to brake master cylinder, wheel cylinder and drum dimensions. The van still had 6-volt electrics and the body was identical to the AKS400. Later in 1972 the AZU250 van was augmented with the 'Grandes Administrations' model with the bigger 435cc engine giving 24bhp at 6,750rpm with its 8.5 compression ratio, breathing through the Solex 34 PICS6 carburettor. The model sported the new 2CV6 gearbox but top speed remained the same at 85km/h. In July 1973 the AKS got a new starter control with 'Command Positive' and in September 1975 the side windows were deleted in the van body, only to reappear two years later when seat belts – non-inertia type – were fitted as standard.

March 1978 saw the disappearance of the AZU and AKS models, and the appearance of the Acadiane van. This was the same idea as the 2CV van but with a Dyane front cab – hence the name 'AK-Dyane'. The front cab roof was slightly higher than the saloon's and the body had door mirrors. The engine was the 602cc, giving 31-bhp at 5,750rpm, with the Solex 26×35CSIC carburettor. Tyres were 135-15X and the platform chassis was the basic AKS unit reinforced and lengthened, which gave an extra 185mm of wheelbase. Payload was up by 40kg and top speed the fastest to date at 100km/h.

# BABY-BROUSSE, DALAT AND FAF VARIANTS

Citroën, ever watchful of world markets, had made sure the 2CV was available in all parts of the world. Local variants were also built by its subsidiary factories: the Citronetta, for example, was built in Chile and was half saloon and half pick-up. Where there was a local transport requirement, there was a version of the 2CV to suit. However, wishing to further aid the peculiar transport needs of some remoter areas of the world, Citroën realized that there was a market for utility vehicles based around existing components, but in a pick-up or Mini Moke style.

The vehicle that resulted Citroën called the Baby-Brousse – *brousse* meaning 'outback' in French. Slab-sided with not a curve in sight, such a vehicle could be assembled in the most basic of manufacturing plants, but could be tough and, with the addition of a folding screen and a fabric roof, be a small load-carrier or saloon car. It was based on the AK van, but was never available in European markets, where its work would

have been catered for by the Méhari. It was made under a manufacturing agreement with Citroën's Iranian subsidiary, SAIPAC. The first Baby-Brousse appeared in 1968. In 1970, at Abidjan on the Ivory Coast, a second plant put the unique utility vehicle into production.

Of even simpler construction and using easy-to-produce flat panels was the Dalat, produced in Saigon in South Vietnam. Again using metal panels rather than the complicated manufacturing processes of the plastic formed panels of the European Méhari, the Dalat is named after a town in South Vietnam; production began in 1970.

(Above) *This impressive special was built by CD Waters in 1948. It was subsequently destroyed by fire – pity.*

*In the Arica zone of Chile, Industrias Citroën Chilena assembled the normal 2CV along with this Citronetta, a saloon with modified semi-pickup bodywork.*

*This 15 Six H Citroën was a one-off specially built by coachbuilders Franay for an unknown ambassador in 1954.*

Launched at the 1978 Dakar Fair, and a much more developed vehicle, is the FAF, which went on to be produced in Senegal and Guinea and was available in kit form in many countries outside Europe. Again using existing components, the FAF was built on a complete 2CV platform chassis, having an estate-style body, again with flat sides and no curves. All seams are welded for ease of production. The letters FAF signify the vehicle's *raison d'être*: *Facile a Fabriquer, Facile a Financier* ('easy to make, easy to finance').

The body could be assembled without machine presses and could therefore be built anywhere with access to accurate welding equipment and fitting shops. The ease of maintenance of the 2CV-based utility vehicle makes it the ideal subject for the trials of use in a poorer country where garage services are simple and basic. The three types sold in reasonable numbers, too, creating employment where they were built. More than 35,000 were made.

Export markets have had other oddities. For example, Iran got a pretty 2CV estate car in 1957, which used standard body parts as far as the central pillars and then had a wooden-framed body at the back. In Chile, the Citronetta appeared in 1963, with station wagon and pick-up variants of the 2CV being built by the Citroën Chilena company in Arica. As for the saloon Citronetta, even that differed from the standard by the addition of a large boot at the rear.

*The UMAP plastic coupe-bodied Citroën 2CV appeared in 1957 at the Paris Salon. Its looks bely the unsurprisingly pedestrian performance.*

## Sahara

(Two engines fitted)

**Engines** (each)

| | |
|---|---|
| Cylinders | Two |
| Cooling | Air |
| Bore and stroke | 66mm × 62mm |
| Capacity | 425cc |
| Compression ratio | 7:1 |
| Carburettors | Solex type 26CBIN controlled by single pedal and relay per cable |
| Max power | 13hp at 4,500rpm (administrative power according to French rating, 5hp) |
| Max torque | 17.6lbft (2.4kg m) at 2,500–3,500rpm |
| Petrol tanks | Two 3.3gal (15ltr) petrol tanks, one per engine, equipped with lamellas immersed filters |
| Petrol pump | Two |

**Transmission**

| | |
|---|---|
| Gearboxes | Four-speed, all synchromesh |
| Clutches | Single dry plate type, hydraulic control with single pedal acting on master cylinder |
| Top gear | 0.679:1 |
| 3rd | 0.516:1 |
| 2nd | 0.308:1 |
| 1st | 0.149:1 |
| Reverse | 0.138:1 |
| Control | Single shift lever controlling the two gearboxes simultaneously. A special coupling lever can shift the gearbox of the rear engine to neutral position in order to drive with the front engine only, for normal road driving |

**Suspension and Steering**

| | |
|---|---|
| Suspension | Oscillating arms on each independent wheel, with longitudinal interactive system |

## Sahara (*continued*)

| | |
|---|---|
| Shock absorbers | Friction type, inertia cylinders |
| Steering gear | Rack-and-pinion. A steering indicator gives the angle of wheels – important for snow, mud and sand driving |
| Tyres | 155 × 400 or 155 × 380 |

### Brakes

| | |
|---|---|
| Type | Hydraulic Lockheed type, acting on all four wheels by means of drums located on the gearboxes, consequently well protected, on rough grounds and very well cooled |
| Surface | 376 cu cm |
| Parking brake | Mechanically operated by hand, acting on front wheels. Security device on the brake handle. It is possible to shift the two gearboxes in first or reverse, as a security for hill parking |

### Electrical System

| | |
|---|---|
| Type | 6-volt |
| Battery | 60A |

### Dimensions

| | |
|---|---|
| Track | 4ft 1⅛in (1,260mm) front and rear |
| Wheelbase | 7ft 10½in (2,405mm) |
| Overall length | 12ft 5in (3,780mm) |
| Overall width | 4ft 10in (1,480mm) |
| Ground clearance | 6⅛in (160mm) |
| Weight dry | 1,576lb (715kg) |
| Weight ready to drive | 1,620lb (735kg), petrol tanks full |
| Maximum weight | 2,293lb (1,040kg) |

### Petrol Consumption

| | |
|---|---|
| With two engines | Approximately 31mpg (9ltr × 100km) on road<br>Approximately 23–28mpg (10–12 ltr × 100km) country driving, according to conditions |
| With one engine | Approximately 47mpg (6ltr × 100km) |

### Accessories

Electric windshield wipers
Bright warning lamp denotes both engines in use
Heater-defroster by the front engine
Air ventilator under windscreen
Reinforced bumpers

Notes
When road driving, it is possible in shifting rear gearbox to neutral position (control device within driver's reach) to drive with only front engine
In case of breakdown it is possible to drive with the rear engine only, by using the special rod furnished with the tools, which keeps the front clutch disengaged

# 6   The Slough 2CVs

Ken Smith was already working at Slough when the 2CV began production there. There were several problems to overcome before the 2CV slotted neatly into volume production, not least the regulations regarding inboard brakes. Smith tells the story:

The 2CV was equipped with inboard front brakes. Motor Vehicles (Construction and Use) Regulations in force in Great Britain until the early Fifties did not permit the use of inboard brakes so that, until the appropriate amendment appeared, it was not possible to assemble the 2CV at Slough for sale in GB. In 1953 the situation changed and the 2CV was introduced.

By this time, production at the Levallois factory had increased to the point where the early body-shell assembly jig had been replaced, and the early jig was made available to the Slough factory. Prior to the arrival of this jig and the acquisition of the associated special-purpose spot-welding equipment a vehicle was required for assessment, and the body-shell of the first vehicle was built without a body-assembly jig, components being assembled on the platform-chassis using body-drawing dimensions, spirit-levels and copper wire diagonal bracing; panel-joints which required specially shaped spot-welding electrodes, not yet available, were secured by

*A photograph by Ken Smith of the first British 2CV. This one was assembled using the Avdel rivet system, before the Slough factory got the spot-welding machines and jigs. It is pictured on the MIRA test track.*

AVDEL aircraft rivets. [During World War Two, Citroën Cars Ltd had made hand-operated riveting-guns in quantity for Aviation Developments Ltd, and still had the prototype.]

France was in full production by the time 2CVs began to be made in Slough. The way we started was to have a French car dismantled and shipped to Slough to decide by pre-assessment how many of the different components and materials we could make or purchase here, and only get from France those items which were expensive in terms of tooling – for example, heavy pressings, engines, gearboxes etc. The dynamo was part of the engine and therefore was made in France. The coil – being double ended and of a particular design – also came from France. All other lamps, lights, wiring, switches and trafficators were obtained in Britain.

Complete components arrived from France. A complete body side – made up of around ten components – arrived complete. There was a jig to assemble the body as a shell, to position the complete sections together. The platform chassis we did consider assembling here, but it was discovered that it would cost more to make here than to have it shipped complete from France.

Behind all this was the consideration that we wanted to reach at least 51 per cent of the final cost price of the car with British content, partly to reduce the amount of duty we paid on importation and also to help our export market where, if we sent a car overseas, to the Commonwealth, those that were deemed British by having 51 per cent British components paid less duty, so there was an advantage. So we strived to increase the British content of the cars. In this was included labour costs, factory costs and rates. We did in the end reach the figures.

The badge on the bonnet of the Slough cars was purely a sales department wish.

They considered it necessary to gain further sales. Unfortunately they incurred the wrath of the French factory because of the weight of it. The script on the bootlid was the same as that for the light Fifteen, as fitted to the spare wheel cover. Seating materials and the seat frames were made here to French specifications. The instruments were also made here. Wilmot Breeden had a door lock which was appropriate. Tyres were supplied by Michelin from Stoke-on-Trent. The hood was pvc-coated knitted cotton material called Everflex. In it we fitted a plastic rear window made of Vybak. This was wider and higher and was secured to the Everflex hood material by an RF welding technique, with an electrode to the window shape and an RF current passed through it from a generator made by Radio Heaters Ltd of Woking. The Vybak and Everflex materials were melted together with this technique. Original French rear windows were of glass. We also introduced a metal bootlid with a lock and a key a long time before the French. The lock on later models worked by locking not the spindle but by unlocking the outside: an early zero-torque lock.

By 1966 the seat belt regulations in this country had made it impossible to sell the 2CV because we had to fit the three-point fixing belts in the front and the centre pillars just had no strength. So from then on there was no way of selling the 2CV legally in this country. There were people who imported them. They were bringing in LHD vehicles of all types. By 1974 the whole car had changed and it was brightened up. They were popular because of the price of petrol at the time.

The Slough 2CVs were more nearly alike to the French direct equivalents than other Citroëns. The Light Fifteen, the six-cylinder models and the DS built at Slough varied to a greater extent than the 2CV.

Motor *photographer Maurice Rowe photographed this 1953 Slough-built 2CV, possibly at Lincoln's Inn Fields in London. Slough cars featured the metal bootlid, more substantial front bumpers and the unique 'front drive' bonnet badge. These glass-plate photographs are of superb quality.*

# 58 MILES to the GALLON !

*The incredible new*

## CITROEN
### 2CV Front Wheel Drive
*Now available as Van or Pick-up*

*The* 2CV **CITROEN** *Front Wheel Drive*

The car with the
**cheapest running costs per mile**
of any four-wheeled four-seater yet produced

### Look at these Features

- Convertible Saloon, weather and draught proof, open or closed at will.
- Full four-seater.
- Four doors.
- Superb suspension.
- Powerful four-wheel brakes.
- Easy to maintain, four greasers only.
  - ● 40 M.P.H.
- Air cooled, no winter precautions necessary.
- Effective heating for the winter and ventilation for summer.
- Easy to drive. Four speeds, all synchronised.
- ROBUST CONSTRUCTION—MADE TO LAST.
  - ● 60 M.P.G.

**The 2 cv contains a host of innovations . . .**

| | |
|---|---|
| ENGINE | 375 c.c., flat twin, air-cooled. Idles almost inaudibly and, of course, needs no anti-freeze precautions in winter. |
| BRAKES | hydraulic brakes on all four wheels. Extremely effective hand-brake operates on transmission. |
| GEARBOX | 3 forward speeds plus overdrive, all synchromesh. |
| COMFORT | removable seats are constructed to give outstanding comfort. The cab can be heated when required by ducts leading from the exhaust manifold. |
| CAPACITY | Van: 66 cu. ft. Pick-up: 32½ cu. ft. (Body Depth 1' 5"). |
| COLOURS | Grey with Red Trim. Sand with Brown Trim. |

THE CITROEN 2CV VAN

THE CITROEN 2CV PICK-UP

**The Little Citroen 2 CV, which caused so many critics to run out of superlatives, is now available as the most economical form of light commercial transport ever to be produced**

### Here are just 4 of its unique characteristics

**ECONOMY—a new word is needed!** The 2 cv is miles-per-gallon ahead of its nearest rivals. Its 58 m.p.g. on lowest grade fuel offers a wonderful reduction in costs to all commercial users. To prevent the driver from forgetting about fuel completely, a red light warns when the last half gallon is reached!

**SPRINGING—'a technical miracle'** The four-wheel independent suspension is completely revolutionary. The 2 cv takes rough ground like a miniature tank. As soon as a front wheel rides a bump, the corresponding rear wheel is automatically prepared to meet the coming shock! Yet, in spite of its remarkable cushioning, there is no tendency to roll or pitch.

**PERFORMANCE—as good as many a 'bus'** Using the Overdrive, the 2 cv will give a tireless 40 m.p.h. over average terrain. One acceleration test yielded 10-50 m.p.h. in 13 secs. . . . carrying a 5 cwt. load and a 17 stone driver! Thanks to front wheel drive and the remarkable suspension, corners can be taken with scarcely any reduction in speed: excellent average speeds are thus achieved on long journeys.

**MAINTENANCE—engineering child's play** Decarbonizing is an easy matter. Four men remove the wing, and the cylinder head can be dismantled within a matter of minutes. The lubrication of engine and chassis is simplicity itself. And, of course, with the air-cooled engine, there is no possibility of 'freezing-up'.

*see it – drive it – and you'll want to own it !*

*The Slough factory put out many enthusiastic brochures such as these, c.1954.*

(Left) *Fuel consumption was nearly up to a heady 60mpg in this brochure.*

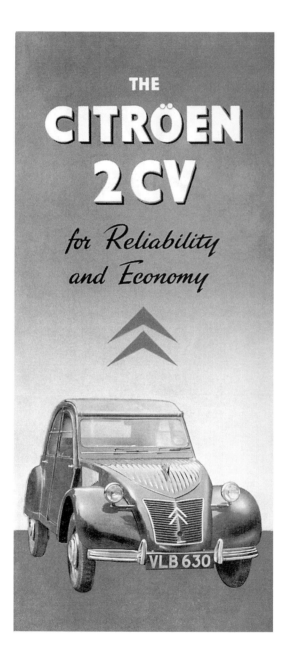

## 2CV PICK-UPS FOR THE ROYAL NAVY

Two batches of specially modified and lightened 2CV Pick-Ups were produced for the Royal Navy in the late 1950s for use in South-East Asia. The vehicles were adapted from the 2CV van and later, quite drastic, weight-saving meant that the Pick-Up could be transported by the Westland Whirlwind helicopters carried on board the aircraft carriers HMS *Bulwark* and HMS *Albion*. They were loaded aboard the two ships in early 1960 and mid-1961, respectively.

The Pick-Ups were adapted by excluding the van body side and top, and cutting the rear panel to level with the box section sides. A drop tailgate was fitted and the cabin itself was enclosed with a special panel made by stretch-forming a sheet of ABOSEDD (Auto Body Sheet Extra Deep Drawing) steel, suitably cut to a defined profile, over a concrete former to provide the basic shape. This was then trimmed and completed by hand. Side panels of the current H-Van were used – suitably swaged – to form the tailgate and the lower cab rear closing panel.

Far from being the same production as the civilian Pick-Up, the Navy version had many special features and changes in its construction; the second batch were even more extensively modified in light of experience in active service: all metal panel joints were pre-treated with a zinc-rich welding primer; two quarter-light glasses were fitted to the rear corners of the cab; two grab handles were fitted to the roof; the petrol filler was extended upwards through the body side to make filling by jerry-can easier, the filler cap itself held by a captive chain; brake pipes and fuel pipes were zinc-plated and coated with chlorinated rubber primer; the windscreen wiper was electrically operated rather than from the

(Above) *HMS* Albion *leaving Portsmouth in November 1962 with full crew on deck. At the rear it carries the 2CV Special Pick-Ups.*

*A Westland Whirlwind of 705 Squadron carries a 2CV van at the Lee-on-Solent Air Day in 1958.*

**Batch 1:**
35 vehicles for HMS *Bulwark*

| | |
|---|---|
| Produced and delivered: | late 1959 to 6 January 1960 |
| Chassis numbers: | 8/596045 to 8/596079 |
| RN Numbers: | 94RN51 to 94RN74 and 94RN92 to 95RN02 |
| Colour specified: | bronze-green enamel DEF 1044VE |

**Batch 2:**
30 vehicles for HMS *Albion*

| | |
|---|---|
| Produced and delivered: | mid-1961 |
| Chassis numbers: | 8/86080 to 8/86109 |
| RN Numbers: | 77RN06 to 77RN35 |
| Paint colour specified: | bronze-green enamel BSC 224 |

*HMS* Albion *entering Hong Kong in 1963 with twenty-six special 2CV Pick-Ups amongst other vehicles on deck.*

speedometer; two warning lamps were fitted to the dash for ignition and oil-pressure; a panoramic interior driving mirror was fitted; bitumen rubber soundproofing sealant was applied to the under-face of platform, interior faces of the wheelarches, spare wheel housing, petrol tank housing, front wings, side floors and body crossmembers; and a fire extinguisher was fitted to the left-hand front toeboard, on a wooden block. All direction indicators were removed, as were wing mirrors. The windscreen glass was fitted with a butyl rubber seal, and all exterior reflective items such as headlamp rims, the scuttle vent aluminium strip and the petrol tank filler cap were painted the bronze-green body colour. The tonneau cover matched the body colour.

Later modifications were effected by Singapore Dockyard. The front number plate was repositioned on to the bonnet; the rear number was removed and painted onto the right-hand rear panel; the front bumper was replaced by a section of angle-iron 9in forward of bonnet grille; the headlamp bar ends were reinforced by welding on a length of strip steel; drain holes were drilled in the forward ends of the cab floor to allow water to escape; a waterproof speedometer was supplied; and a water deflector for the ammeter was fitted. (These last two were for vehicles operated with the windscreen removed.)

In the tropical climates where the Pick-Ups were mostly used the following items were permanently removed: side doors, passenger seat, rubber mat, petrol tank and spare wheel cover panels, windscreen and rear cab glass, windscreen wiper, tonneau cover and fire extinguisher. These removals

*A Westland Wessex about to lift a Citroën 2CV 'truck' – registration number 94 RN 97 – from HMS* Bulwark *in March 1961.*

*A Westland Whirlwind of 845 Squadron lifts a 2CV Special with registration number 33 CPP. The lifting cable is looped through the handles below the tail opening and under the body.*

reduced the vehicle weight by 190lb. The removal of the screen glass also eliminated reflections which could have revealed the vehicle to a distant observer. At the reduced weight, it was possible for a few troops to lift the vehicle out of any tight corners.

During the period between the two batches, the standard 2CV tyres – 135 × 400 – were replaced by 135 × 380; the earlier type had been found to puncture frequently in the rough conditions experienced by the Navy versions. Tests were made with a sturdier 5.00/5.60 15N tyre, but as there were problems of increased turning circle and fouling of the wheelarches, these tyres were not fitted.

## BIJOU

Citroën's many overseas branches have from time to time produced variations of the company's basic models to suit local conditions which were never made available in France. Of particular interest to Citroën enthusiasts in Britain is the *Bijou* ('jewel') model which was introduced in 1960.

The 'Jewel' of Slough, if it can be called that, should have worked. These days it would sell like hot cakes with its 'retro' styling and charming looks, but at the time it was expensive, heavy and slow. The seats fitted to the Bijou were not 2CV seats and were less comfortable. In fact, the driving position was uncomfortable, too, with the steering wheel – a single-spoke type taken from the DS – set too high. Consciously designed to resemble some styling ideas of the DS, the Bijou used many parts from that model including door handles, window winders and some of the other controls. It did employ 2CV inner front wings. In the end the body weighed nearly 2cwt more than the standard 2CV. It was the only all-Slough-built special Citroën, only the engines and inner wings coming from France.

The story of the Bijou is recalled by Ken Smith, Chief Engineer at Slough at the time:

The Bijou was a well-intentioned move. The 2CV at the time was not selling well, and sales manager Nigel Somerset-Leeke went to Managing Director Louis Garbe and suggested that a new design with a nice-shaped body which was light and aerodynamic would sell. Garbe in turn would have to get agreement from the parent company in France. M. Bercot, who was

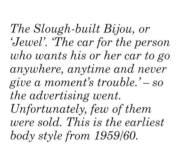

*The Slough-built Bijou, or 'Jewel'. 'The car for the person who wants his or her car to go anywhere, anytime and never give a moment's trouble.' – so the advertising went. Unfortunately, few of them were sold. This is the earliest body style from 1959/60.*

*The Bijou's rear end had something of the Renault Dauphine about it. In these days of retro styling the Bijou would sell well. In 1961, sadly, it did not.*

117

*The 1961 Bijou had a slightly modified front end and revised bodywork.*

*This heavily retouched photograph shows the DS and Ami-type of single spoke steering wheel in use on the Bijou. Only 211 were made in four years.*

President Director General, agreed that Slough could make this effort on its own without occupying any of the time of the Bureau d'Etudes, because it already had a full workload. Bercot was interested to see what sort of result the Slough factory could produce on its own without the benefit of all their experts.

The body designer who had made the Lotus Elite, Peter Kirwan-Taylor, was contracted to design the Bijou body. The idea was to have a vehicle that had some family resemblance to the DS. The job of producing the moulds went to a company in West Drayton which had some experience of making plastic body cabs for lorries. It was, however, early days in the technology of glass-fibre car bodies and there were many problems in assembling the Bijou. It was

not the cakewalk it was intended to be. After 102 bodyshells, manufacture was transferred to a firm in Crowthorne. But even here, where they tried every possible way of producing the bodies, the overall result was not as economical as one would have wanted. The exercise started in 1959, came to production in 1960 and continued until 1964 – all to build 211 cars. It was one headache less when we dropped it.

The Bijou's problem was its cost. At £695 5s 10d for the basic car in 1961, it was more expensive than the Ford Popular, Prefect and Anglia, the Morris Minor 1000, the Austin A35 and A40, and the BLMC Minis. Unfortunately, the British public shunned the little Bijou. The few that are left are collectors' items today.

---

### Slough-built 2CV (1953)

**Engine**

| | |
|---|---|
| Cylinders | Two |
| Cooling | Air |
| Bore and stroke | 62 × 62mm |
| Capacity | 375cc |
| Piston area | 9.36sq in |
| Valves | Pushrod OHV |
| Compression ratio | 6.2:1 |
| Carburettor | Solex downdraught |
| Maximum power | 9bhp at 3,500rpm |
| Piston speed at max bhp | 1,425ft per min |
| Ignition | 6-volt coil |
| Sparking plugs | KLG FA50 14mm |
| Fuel pump | Mechanical |
| Oil filter | Gauze on pump |

**Transmission**

| | |
|---|---|
| Clutch | Single dry plate |
| Top gear | 5.72:1 |
| 3rd | 7.50:1 |
| 2nd | 12.55:1 |
| 1st | 25.90:1 |
| Final drive | Spiral bevel |

**Slough-built 2CV (1953)** (*continued*)

**Suspension and Steering**

| | |
|---|---|
| Suspension | All wheels independently sprung, by leading arms at front and trailing arms at rear. Central coil springs coupled to both front and rear wheels |
| Shock absorbers | Oil-damped units on each wheel to check patter |
| Steering gear | Rack-and-pinion |
| Turning circle | 33ft (10.06m) |
| Turns, lock to lock | 2.5 |
| Tyres | Michelin 125 × 400 |

**Brakes**

| | |
|---|---|
| Type | Lockheed hydraulic (front brakes on differential assembly) |
| Brake drum diameter | 7½in (190.5mm) |
| Friction lining area | 60.9sq in (393sq cm) |

**Dimensions**

| | |
|---|---|
| Wheelbase | 7ft 9¼in (2,369mm) |
| Overall length | 12ft 5in (3,785mm) |
| Overall width | 4ft 10½in (1,486mm) |
| Overall height | 5ft 3in (1,600mm) |
| Ground clearance | 7½in (190.5mm) |
| Unladen kerb weight | 10cwt (508kg) |

**Performance**

| | |
|---|---|
| Maximum speed | 40.9mph (65.8km/h) |
| Fastest | 42.3mph (68.1km/h) |
| Acceleration | 0–30mph 19.6sec |
| | 0–40mph 42.4sec |
| | Standing quarter mile (0.4km) 43.4sec |
| Fuel consumption | 76mpg (3.73ltr × 100km) at constant 20mph |
| | 75mpg (3.77ltr × 100km) at constant 30mph |
| | 70mpg (4.04ltr × 100km) at constant 35mph |
| | 54.7mpg (5.17ltr × 100km) overall |
| Price | £398 (£564 19s 2d including purchase tax) |

**Differences for 1954**

**Transmission**

| | |
|---|---|
| Clutch | Single dry plate clutch, 160mm diameter (6.3in) |
| Top gear | 5.7:1 |
| 3rd gear | 7.5:1 |
| 2nd gear | 2.55:1 |
| 1st gear | 25.9:1 |
| Reverse | 28.1:1 |
| Final drive | Spiral bevel, with a ratio of 3.87:1. Needle roller universal jointed shafts to the front wheels |

**Slough-built 2CV (1953)** (*continued*)

**Suspension and Steering**

| | |
|---|---|
| Suspension | Single leading arms on each side at the front and trailing arms at the rear. Coil-type, compression springs are incorporated in an interconnecting link between the front and rear arms on each side |
| Shock absorbers | A dynamic absorber of Citroën design mounted on each wheel hub |
| Steering gear | Rack-and-pinion, 2¼ turns from lock to lock |
| Turning circle | 35ft 6in (10.82m) to left and 35ft 3in (10.74m) to right |

**Brakes**

| | |
|---|---|
| Type | Lockheed hydraulic leading and trailing shoe brakes at front and rear |
| Drum diameters | Front 7.8in (198mm), rear 7.87in (199.9mm) |
| Shoe width | 1.55in (39.4mm) |

**Dimensions**

| | |
|---|---|
| Track | 4ft 1⅝in (1,260mm) front and rear |
| Wheelbase | 7ft 9⁵⁄₁₆in (2,370mm) |
| Overall length | 12ft 4¾in (3,778mm) |
| Overall width | 4ft 10³⁄₁₆in (1,478mm) |
| Overall height | 5ft 3in (1,600mm) |
| Ground clearance | 7½in (190.5mm) |
| Unladen weight | 1,100lb (500kg) |
| Unladen weight distribution | Front 58.8 per cent, rear 41.2 per cent |
| Price | £398 (£564 19s 2d including purchase tax) |

**Slough-built 2CV AZ (1956)**

**Engine**

| | |
|---|---|
| Cylinders | Two |
| Cooling | Air |
| Bore and stroke | 66mm × 62mm |
| Capacity | 425cc |
| Piston area | 10sq in |
| Valves | Inclined pushrod OHV |
| Compression ratio | 6.2:1 |
| Carburettor | Solex downdraught |
| Max power | 12bhp at 3,500rpm |
| Piston speed at max bhp | 1,420ft per min |
| Ignition | Duplex coil |
| Sparking plugs | Champion H9 |
| Fuel pump | Mechanical |

| Slough-built 2CV AZ (1956) *(continued)* | |
|---|---|
| Oil filter | Gauze on pump |
| Fuel tank capacity | 4½gal (20.5ltr) |

**Transmission**

| | |
|---|---|
| Clutches | Single dry plate and centrifugal clutches in series |
| Top gear | 5.7:1 |
| 3rd | 7.5:1 |
| 2nd | 12.55:1 |
| 1st | 25.9:1 |
| Final drive | 8:31 spiral bevel |
| Top gear at 1,000rpm | 11.9mph (19km/h) |
| Top gear at 1,000ft/min piston speed | 29.2mph (47km/h) |

**Suspension and Steering**

| | |
|---|---|
| Suspension | Independent front and rear, by interconnected leading and trailing arms with coil springs in compression below centre of car |
| Shock absorbers | Inertia 'patter' dampers on wheels and friction damping on suspension arm pivots |
| Steering gear | Rack-and-pinion |
| Turning circle between kerbs | Left 32ft 9in (9.98m), right 32ft 3in (9.83m) |
| Turns, lock to lock | 2¼ |
| Tyres | Michelin 125 × 400 |

**Brakes**

| | |
|---|---|
| Type | Lockheed hydraulic |
| Brake drum diameter | Front 7.9in (200.7mm), rear 7.1in (180.3mm) |
| Friction lining area | 60.9sq in (393sq cm) |

**Dimensions**

| | |
|---|---|
| Track | 4ft 1⅜in (1,254mm) front and rear |
| Wheelbase | 7ft 9¼in (2,369mm) |
| Overall length | 12ft 4¾in (3,778mm) |
| Overall width | 4ft 10¼in (1,480mm) |
| Overall height | 5ft 3in (1,600mm) |
| Ground clearance | 7½in (190.5mm) |

**Performance**

| | |
|---|---|
| Maximum speed | 47.2mph (76km/h) |
| Fastest | 49.2mph (79.2km/h) |
| Acceleration | 0–20mph 6.3sec |
| | 0–30mph 13.6sec |
| | 0–40mph 27sec |
| | Standing quarter mile (0.4km) 31.1sec |
| Fuel consumption | 76.5mpg (3.69ltr × 100km) at constant 20mph (32.2km/h) |

**Slough-built 2CV AZ (1956)** (*continued*)

70.5mpg (4.0ltr × 100km) at constant 30mph (48.3km/h)
59mpg (4.79ltr × 100km) at constant 40mph (64.4km/h)
49.7mpg (5.68ltr × 100km) overall

**Equipment**

| | |
|---|---|
| Tools | Starting handle |
| | Bevel-type jack (two jacking points on each side of body) |
| | Wheelbrace |
| | Chock |
| | Radiator muff |
| | Dipstick |
| | Two double-ended spanners |
| | Box spanner |
| | Screwdriver |
| | Pliers |
| Exterior lights | Two dipping headlamps with pilot bulbs |
| | Two tail lamps |
| | Number plate lamp |
| Direction indicators | Semaphore-type, self cancelling |
| Windscreen wipers | Two-blade mechanical, driven from speedometer cable with handle for manual operation. |
| Sun visors | One universally pivoted |
| Instruments | Speedometer with non-trip |
| | Non-decimal distance recorder |
| | Ammeter |
| Warning lights | Low fuel level |
| Locks | Ignition |
| | Driver's door and luggage locker one key |
| Parcel shelf | Full width across facia |
| Ashtray | One in front |
| Interior lights | One above windscreen, also serving as speedometer light |
| Interior heater | Fresh-air type with separate intake of cold air for demisting screen |
| Extras | Fog lamp |
| Upholstery | Plastic |
| Floor covering | Rubber |
| Exterior colours | Grey or red |
| | |
| Price | £398 (£598 7s including purchase tax) |

## Bijou

**Engine**

| | |
|---|---|
| Cylinders | Two |
| Cooling | Air |
| Bore and stroke | 66mm × 62mm |
| Capacity | 425cc |
| Valves | OHV, push rod operated |
| Compression ratio | 7.00:1 |
| Carburettor | Downdraught with intake air filter and silencer |
| Max power | 12bhp at 3,500rpm |
| Fuel pump | Mechanical |
| Ignition | Coil |
| Fuel tank capacity | 4½gal (20.5ltr) |

**Transmission**

| | |
|---|---|
| Gearbox | Four-speed |
| Clutch | Single dry disc |
| Top gear | 5.7:1 |
| 3rd | 7.5:1 |
| 2nd | 12.56:1 |
| 1st | 25.91:1 |

**Suspension and Steering**

| | |
|---|---|
| Suspension | Independent Citroën on all four wheels |
| Steering gear | Rack-and-pinion |
| Turning circle | 35ft 6in (10.82m) |
| Tyres | Michelin 135 × 15 (135 × 380) |

**Brakes**

| | |
|---|---|
| Type | Hydraulic (front inboard) |

**Dimensions**

| | |
|---|---|
| Track | 4ft 1⅝in (1,260mm) |
| Wheelbase | 7ft 9¼in (2,369mm) |
| Overall length | 12ft 11in (3,937mm) |
| Overall width | 5ft 2in (1,575mm) |
| Overall height | 4ft 10in (1,473mm) |
| Ground clearance (unladen) | 7½in (190.5mm) |

Bijou chassis numbers start at 8/600101 in 1960, and end at 8/600313 in 1964

**A-Model production at Slough**

**2CV Saloon 1953–60**

| Model Year | Type | Chassis Nos | Production |
|---|---|---|---|
| 1953 | A | 8/530001–8/530026 | 26 |
| 1954 | A | 8/530027–8/530176 | 150 |
| 1955 | A | 8/530177–8/530186 | 10 |
| 1955 | AZ | 8/551001–8/551177 | 177 |
| 1956 | AZ | 8/561001–8/561061 | 61 |
| 1957 | AZ | 8/571062–8/571126 | 65 |
| 1958 | AZ | 8/581127–8/581207 | 81 |
| 1959 | AZ | 8/591208–8/591288 | 81 |
| 1960 | AZ | 8/601289–8/601309 | 21 |

Sales: Home 330; Export 342    Total 672

**2CV Van 1953–60**

| Model Year | Type | Chassis Nos | Production |
|---|---|---|---|
| 1953 | AU | 8/537001–8/537003 | 3 |
| 1954 | AU | 8/537004–8/537069 | 66 |
| 1955 | AU | 8/537070–8/537081 | 12 |
| 1955 | AZU | 8/558001–8/558052 | 52 |
| 1956 | AZU | 8/568001–8/568013 | 13 |
| 1957 | AZU | 8/578014–8/578032 | 19 |
| 1958 | AZU | 8/588033–8/588054 | 22 |
| 1959 | AZU | 8/598055–8/598072 | 18 |
| 1960 | AZU | 8/608073–8/608098 | 26 |

Sales: Home 84; Export 147    Total 231

Slough A-Model production grand total: 1,245

**2CV Pick-up 1953–61**

| Model Year | Type | Chassis Nos | Production |
|---|---|---|---|
| 1953 | AP | 8/535001 | 1 |
| 1954 | AP | 8/535002–8/535005 | 4 |
| 1955 | AP | 8/535006–8/535012 | 7 |
| 1955 | AZP | 8/556001–8/556010 | 10 |
| 1956 | AZP | 8/566001–8/566009 | 9 |
| 1957 | AZP | 8/576010–8/576019 | 10 |
| 1958 | AZP | 8/586020–8/586043 | 24 |
| 1959 | AZP | 8/596044 | 1 |
| 1960 | AZP (RN) | 8/596045–8/596079 | 35 |
| 1961 | AZP (RN) | 8/86080–8/86109 | 30 |

Sales: Home 131; Export 0    Total 131

**2CV Bijou 1960–64**

| Model Year | Type | Chassis Nos | Production |
|---|---|---|---|
| 1960 | BJ | 8/600101–8/600163 | 63 |
| 1961 | BJ | 8/600164–8/600184 | 21 |
| 1962 | BJ | 8/600185–8/600241 | 57 |
| 1963 | BJ | 8/600242–8/600269 | 28 |
| 1964 | BJ | 8/600270–8/600311 | 42 |

Sales: Home 207; Export 4    Total 211

# 7 Media Reaction to the 2CV

*The Motor* of 19 October 1949, perhaps unwittingly, put its finger on the *raison d'être* of the Deux Chevaux when, in one of the first reports about the new model to appear in the British press, it wrote:

> Among the most interesting post-war projects from France is the 2CV Citroën, an extreme economy model designed to supplement the range of fast family cars produced by the same manufacturers. It is a car which is not merely planned to be exceptionally inexpensive to manufacture and economical of fuel; it is also intended to have that rugged simplicity of mechanical and electrical detail which will allow it to withstand extremes of abuse and neglect in any part of the world.

In 1953, the same journal wrote of the Deux Chevaux, now built in Slough, that it was, 'A vehicle with almost every virtue except speed, silence and good looks'.

This condescending phrase was, however, about as critical as *The Motor* got in its road test of 30 December 1953. In particular, it praised the ingenious and unique suspension:

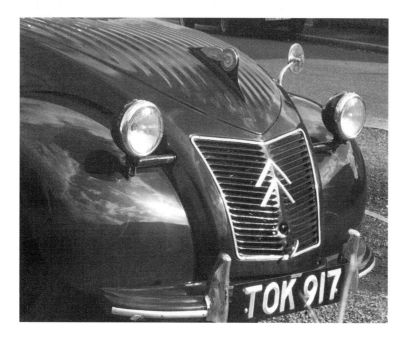

*Slough-built cars sported the heavy 'Front Drive' mascot, bonnet mounted.*

Without doubt the most striking single feature of the Citroën is the riding comfort achieved by the unique system of independent suspension. Unsprung weight has been reduced to a minimum by using very light wheels on leading and trailing arms, while the front brakes are mounted inboard. Front and rear wheels on each side are interconnected through a cylinder containing two coil springs, and have an exceptionally long and flexible travel. The soft-ness of the suspension is apparent from the change of attitude of the car when loaded with varying numbers of passengers. On the road its effectiveness is proved by a ride which is excellent even by big-car standards. Ordinary cobbled surfaces go unnoticed, and an unmade, heavily pot-holed road which strikes something akin to terror into the hearts of local residents was taken at 30mph. Moreover, there is very little road noise.

*Early publicity shots of the new Citroën usually showed the new model in rural or holiday settings, as befitted its intended market.*

*The rural publicity continues with this 1955 2CV AZ and family.*

*Motor World* of 22 May 1953 tried to pigeon-hole the Deux Chevaux, but found it difficult:

> Comparison of the 2CV with other automobiles is difficult. Economical, safe and dependable, it does not attempt to create the false impression of being a luxury model at low cost. It is a new kind of car, or at least represents a type which has been out of production for a long time – perhaps too long.

*Motor World* went on to describe the little car's popularity:

> Since then [the launch in 1949] the 2CV has confounded its critics. It has become the rage of Paris, as well as of the hinterlands. The measure of its success can be easily discovered. Try to buy one. The waiting list is longer than that for any other car.

While the Deux Chevaux had been around for a good few years in France it was relatively new in Britain, and it was not until April 1954 that *Motor Sport* published the results of an extended test of over 2,000 miles, including some hillclimbing in Wales, in the 'Citroën Cyclecar' as they called it:

Petrol economy is one of the highlights of the 2CV. It really is rather ridiculous. For example, when the car was delivered to the Motor Sport office I was told that it had a full tank. Leaving on the Thursday afternoon I used the car almost continuously, and hard, until the tank ran dry on the Monday morning. I had during this time added only two gallons, so the consumption was obviously approximately 60mpg. Intrigued, I then tested with two gallons of cheap petrol, using the car though London to the office, driving it hard on the open road, up hilly country in Sussex which brought it frequently down to bottom gear, over roads heavy with snow and slush, including starting it on the Tuesday morning on the choke – result 60.1mpg. The overall mpg from there until the test concluded, 2,075 miles and many Welsh gradients later, was 59.9. There is no possible doubt, therefore, that under favourable average conditions the 2CV betters 60mpg. Indeed, coasting on hills, but still with a number of choke-starts, seventy-two miles were covered on one gallon.

*Swiss plates are on this Belgium-built 2CV which has the rear flashing indicators mounted on the rear wings.*

*Motor Sport* went on to describe the Welsh weekend with a glowing report on the Citroën:

> Thirty years ago, away back in 1924, the RAC ran a Six-Days Trial for Small Cars over a punishing course in Wales. The cars had to be standard models, they lost marks for stopping and shedding passengers on hills, for any time required for repairs, adjustments or taking up the brakes, they were timed up some very steep 'Welsh Alps' and were bucketed and buffeted over vile Welsh by-roads and mountain tracks. After five days of this they were timed up the old Birdlip Hill in Gloucestershire, after which they proceeded to Brooklands Track for acceleration and speed tests and an examination for general mechanical condition ... I had long wanted to look at the course used for this 1924 contest and the 2CV Citroën seemed just the car for the job. It would, I thought, be instructive to see whether a 375cc 10cwt small car of 1954 would do what a 950cc 13cwt light car accomplished in 1924.

Snowfall, torrential rain and closed roads meant that the crew couldn't complete the exact route, but the author was nevertheless jubilant about the performance of the 2CV:

> This excursion into Wales set the seal to my already favourable opinion of the baby Citroën. It is a fascinating, splendid little car, to which I would gladly give permanent shelter in my garage. Its designer, who must be a brilliant engineer indeed, has approached fearlessly the problem of providing a modern people's car. His solution bears out the plea I have made so frequently in Motor Sport – use a truly small engine and real economy will follow. The 2CV's 'square' flat-twin is astonishingly smooth, not unduly noisy, does not indulge in vices, and seems to be unburstable. It returns the fuel consumption its makers claim, which is almost unique in my experience.

Praise indeed!

*Of course it wasn't only families to which the 2CV appealed: the younger set were also buyers. This is an AZL model.*

*The Autocar* of 22 January 1954 perhaps started the trend of using a 2CV for the hardest driving trials. To this day the 2CV has been used to drive round the world, even across the Sahara, and in this report from Buckinghamshire to John O'Groats, and then back to Land's End during a cold and foggy December:

> Whoever was driving had to work for his living and more or less pump the gear lever like a fireman on an express locomotive shovelling coal. This gear-changing business is quite a feature of the 2CV. A little tricky to start with perhaps, as more than once second was engaged instead of over-drive, but the designer must have had people like us in mind, as there have been no ill feelings from the gearbox. Having got the idea, it is possible to make very rapid changes and to use the limit markings on the speedometer rather like a rev counter; only, instead of taking care not to go over the limits, it was found essential to maintaining our selfset average not to drop below the limit and the engine seemed to thrive on this treatment.

The intrepid crew reached John O'Groats in 26 hr 10min which, excluding stops, averages at 32.8mph. On their return to the Buckinghamshire village of Frieth from where they had set out, the little Citroën had covered 1,593 miles, averaged 57mpg and had only been overtaken by fifty-eight other vehicles. The writer summed up:

> An amazing car in its way, most unattractive to look at, very cleverly designed by men who are not afraid of the unorthodox, most efficient and stronger than it appears. It can cover the ground not too slowly and is more comfortable than some cars which cost three or four times the price. It will operate off the beaten track if need be, and

indeed an example has already been seen in the Sahara heading for darkest Africa. It will carry four heavy people without too much reduction of performance, and still climb stoutly in second gear, and the ability of the suspension to deal with a rough track which one would hesitate to take at all in an ordinary car is almost uncanny. The 2CV just floats over such surfaces on an even keel.

The onward journey to Land's End was conducted with the 2CV, fully laden with Christmas gifts and extra passengers. It had now been christened *Kon Tiki*, by a sleeping off-duty driver dreaming of a journey to Cornwall on the *Kon Tiki* raft fitted with an outboard motor:

> Full throttle down hills, up hills, on the level and even a good part of the time in built-up areas gave drivers and passenger alike a feeling of pressing on. Thus on a long night journey, which terminated in the small hours, there was much less feeling of impatience than might be expected of people accustomed to normally powered cars. And, which is remarkable, there was no feeling of travel-tiredness after a thoroughly restful journey.
>
> Altogether, 11.5 gallons of petrol were consumed, and a pint of oil. For a total outlay of a little over 50s three people had travelled 575 miles at a fuel consumption of 50mpg – a cost of 17s per head as opposed to the £4-odd of a return ticket by rail. This abnormally small thirst, if not the most important, is one of the greater joys of an intriguing little car.

The writer rounded off his piece with this epilogue:

> Very definitely do its singular qualities grow on one. At first the contrast with the

*This shot shows the extreme simplicity of the hood fixing. This is a later six-light model.*

average car in every single respect, and of course in performance, may prove slightly repellent. But make a journey with the 2CV, sample it for the handy runabout that it is, so easily parked, for a few days and you are apt to become a convert. On a main road journey if time presses it may be tedious, but a sense of achievement and of regard and respect for the car's unique character is likely to prevail. The affection develops for a car, especially a small one, with which one has been places.

The Australian car magazine *Wheels* of November 1955 commented on the bigger-engined 2CV:

The new model goes wonderfully well on the road. The sound-proofing gives a considerable reduction in noise from the earlier model, and in fact brings the noise level down almost enough to make it comparable with other small cars.

The centrifugal clutch does away with the use of the clutch when starting from rest. It is set to take up at 700rpm. First gear can thus be engaged without the use of the clutch because the engine idles below 700rpm.

The car is moved off the line by depressing the accelerator. As the revs build up the clutch engages, and you move off. An anti-stalling device fitted to the throttle linkage, combined with the clutchless take-off, makes the car ridiculously easy to drive.

The Citroën can be braked to a stop in any of its gears because the centrifugal clutch throws out when engine revs drop below 700rpm.

*Wheels* summed up the new Citroën:

> Make no mistake, this small car has everything right down to a heater and self-cancelling trafficators. Even the dust seal is good.
>
> Stark and different as it is, it has a definite appeal once one is used to its look. It has an almost narcotic effect on the technically minded because of the number of brilliant engineering ideas.
>
> In conclusion we must say that we will not be impressed with any other economy car's petrol consumption until it can better the Citroën 2CV's amazing thrift.

*Slough cars had the Lucas trafficators fitted ahead of the front doors.*

*The Motor* of 25 January 1956 was impressed with the AZ model's go-anywhere capabilities:

> Despite its low power and front-wheel drive this is very much a go-anywhere car, the Michelin tyres gripping well in mud or snow – if all else fails, this model can, when unladen, be reversed up altogether abnormally steep and slippery hills which would defeat an orthodox saloon, not exhibiting the strong reverse castor effect on the steering which makes this emergency procedure impracticable on some heavier front-drive cars. Suitability of this model for unmade roads or for use across country is emphasised by suspension which is abnormally flexible and permits astonishingly large wheel deflections without 'bottoming'.

In a piece entitled 'One of the Family', *The Autocar* of 25 May 1956, gave space for a 'Feminine Assessment', perhaps unwittingly acknowledging the popularity the 2CV was to gain with women.

> The wheels turned off the road and jogged happily up a commonland path, wide enough to take two walkers abreast; then the car clambered up and down some springy anthills, no more shock than a soft rise and fall of the body being felt by the occupants. This is the chief joy of the 2CV for the ride through the utility type rubber-sprung seats feels a though one is swinging in a hammock suspended by the four corners (each wheel is independently sprung) and the occupants ride along gently, with dents in the road surface transforming themselves into waves of progress.
>
> One feels at home in the driving seat immediately, although it was some time before I was used to the organ-type throttle pedal – long enough to take a man-size foot – in the way it was meant to be used, for it

seemed more natural to let a high heel slip down beside the device and rest on the floor. Because the car is so light the brakes act very quickly. The urge transmitted by two cylinders and 12bhp is rarely enough to make crash stops necessary.

It is a common fallacy – as far as I am concerned, anyway – that women are endowed with a greater share of patience than men. However the jaunty gait of the 2CV soon dissipates fret and worry for male and female alike; you can't overtake as though this were a thrusting sports car – not unless you have a clear road well ahead and the vehicle in front is a lumbering lorry. Instead, you can sit back and delight in the thought of 425cc under the sloping corrugated bonnet. This example was finished in maroon.

The wheel feels strange at first, and I found myself oversteering drastically, but it is only a matter of getting used to the unique independent suspension.

The gear lever is at facia height, and the movement has to be studied carefully at first. There is a comfortably large knob

*Forward opening doors had advantages – but for safety were dropped later.*

*All manufacturers liked to prepare chassis cutaways, and Citroën was no exception.*

forming the top of the lever which disappears into the parcel shelf, and this twists to the left, for reverse and first; to centre, 2nd and 3rd; and to the right for overdrive.

Engagement is precise, the only snag being the change down from overdrive (a quiet coasting gear for main road journeys) into second, for the lever must pass through third position to get there. It is great fun to nurse the 2CV along, changing frequently, and whipping it gently up to something approaching a triumphant 50mph on a down slope, and even then not flat out. The car is at its happiest around 40 – a very restful speed.

Feminine approval must, I think, be witheld from the external system checking petrol – a very long and willowy dipstick, in brick-coloured plastic, which appears like the conjuror's rabbit from underneath the fuel filler cap. Because the petrol evaporates so rapidly from the stick it is rather difficult to tell how much has been used. But there is also a warning light inside the car which glows red when petrol is dangerously low, and you can depend upon it that the 20 litres which the tank holds will disappear very slowly indeed, and the driver with foresight need not always be getting out to see if there is enough petrol.

There is a lot of room inside the body shell, and when the driving seat is right back, the rear passenger can sit easily without wishing he could telescope his legs. A surprising amount of luggage space, for a car of this class, is hidden behind the back seats with the spare wheel.

In the summer a hood of Everflex (a synthetic leather-type material) can be pulled back, but there are a few fears of the cold winter air taking advantage of this, for the interior is heated to a tolerable temperature.

The interior light is similar in shape to an upturned ginger beer bottle and it spotlights the lovely speedometer; at the same time the centre section can be twisted to reveal the bulb, and it can be put to full or half position according to how much interior illumination is required. This is just one of several endearing details which make a woman long to get a duster and rub the 2CV's bonnet shiny.

American magazine *Motor Trend* of February 1957 succinctly put into words the extraordinary gait of the 2CV:

Upshifts can be made as smooth as an Olympic skier changing direction in a slalom, or as jerky as a kayak shooting the rapids. If you keep your foot on it while shifting, the car will crouch, then leap like a gazelle as the clutch takes hold. Keeping up your speed will be a matter of necessity in traffic and on hills. Here, everything from a Ford Model A in stock condition on up will show you its tail feathers.

But author Walt Woron was philosophic about the 2CV's true appeal:

To put up with the 2CVs idiosyncrasies, you have to enjoy life. You also have to be able to laugh at the leers and jeers of fellow motorists. But, if you want a car to have fun with, that you can practically disassemble in a matter of minutes, that seats four persons in extreme comfort, that gives 35–45mpg in town driving, then don't laugh too loudly at the 2CV. It does all these things – and for only $1,350–$1,395.

The strangely-titled *Popular Imported Cars* of November 1970 also netted the philosophy angle:

This is not a car, its a philosophy. To properly drive a 2CV you must be French – if you're an outlander take heart though – French driving can be self taught. Or rather

*1969 models had improved bumpers with rubber strips applied to the overriders.*

learned from all the helpful comments hurled at you when you stray from the one true way. The first thing you learn as you hit rush hour traffic in Paris is about acceleration. You let the clutch out in first and wonder, a) if you are in gear at all, b) if it is a forward gear. By and by the car moves off then comes the next step – shifting. You push in the clutch and grapple with a very firm lever sticking out of the dash. A bit of strength and a bit of faith and you are in second, third comes easy after that unless a light, policemen, traffic jam or some other charming impediment has placed itself firmly in your path. If such has happened you push the brakes. And you stop.

The author was beginning to get the hang of it:

Back in Paris the traffic was easy now. Had the car improved? No, we had just learned to drive it. The tendency to keep any velocity achieved was evident as we brushed back an old lady trying to cross against the light. Our passenger complained that we were driving like a Frenchman. This pleased us because now we understood how a Frenchman could love this car. And this understanding passes to other areas like strong cheese, strange politics and a better understanding of the French mentality. Driving the 2CV won't give you a better grade in your French classes but it will help you when you are in trouble.

Under the subtitle 'Liberty, practicality, ecology', *Wheels* magazine of May 1974 proclaimed 'Vive le Deux Chevaux' in an article

*This 1970 base model still featured the simple metal two-spoke steering wheel.*

addressing the then-current fears of a fuel crisis and the ecological viewpoint of car ownership:

> The 2CV is not defined by what it is (fast, luxurious or smart) but by what it is not (expensive, petrol thirsty, garish or complicated). Its buyer is conscious of acquiring something different from what is usually expected of a car.
>
> For this very reason it is a statusless vehicle. Originally aimed at the French middle classes, it has become accepted as something else – a way of life, an outlook, a philosophy. Its styling, if it can be called that, pre-supposes nothing. In just over twenty-five years of mass production, no dictates of fashion have influenced the basic shape ... the 2CV is as much part of the [Paris] scene as a bread roll ... The 2CV has become the accepted symbol of

the alternative society, or simply of those concerned with reliability, economy and function before fashion and finesse. And today those qualities make it the Best Car in the World.

*Autocar's* Road Test of 8 March 1975 told us:

> It is easy enough to put the 2CV into perspective: there is simply nothing else quite like it. We chose our competitors for the comparison tables on the basis that they were minimum-cost motoring, but none of them have the same kind of personality – though all have personalities of their own (Hillman Imp, Renault 4L, Mini 850, Fiat 126). If you want the same kind of car, the only alternative is to stay with Citroën and spend another £90 on the Dyane 6 to gain better styling and seat comfort, but sacrifice some minimal running costs.

It is running costs which remain the basic *raison d'être* of the 2CV's existence. On the evidence of this test, direct operating costs are about as low as you will find on four wheels. Purchase price is low, but it remains to be seen if the car can establish a sufficient market for itself to hold a reasonable second-hand value. Apart from that, how does it rate as a car? Remarkably well in most respects. If there were two areas where we would look for improvement, it would be in wind noise and seat design. But as it stands, the 2CV is the archetypal car of the age – the answer to the energy crisis.

*Alloy wing finishers – or protectors – were made as period accessories by Robri.*

Michael Bowler in *The Motor* of 5 July 1975 wrote his impressions of a 2CV6 after 12,000 miles:

In 1936 Pierre Boulanger, Citroën's Managing Director, gave his designers instructions to build 'an umbrella on four wheels'. An economical and reliable vehicle which can transport four people and 110lb of luggage at 35mph in the maximum comfort.

Thankfully the 35mph design brief is long surpassed, as anyone who's driven in France knows, and the comfort level is still of a very high order as you may have observed by the speeds the little Citroëns maintain on broken byways. Some 12,000 miles after our acquisition of the staff 2CV6 we have had every reason to be grateful to a car that has given remarkably little trouble, saved us a lot of money and provided ever-ready transport to a number of people whose normal vehicles have not been notable for reliability.

*Road & Track* of May 1985 mixed philosophy with driving impressions of the Charleston model:

The 2CV6 is so basic that you quickly realise it's the only true car in the world. All other automobiles are really *rolling environments* – townhouses, offices, boudoirs, spacelabs, whatever – while the Duck [as the magazine had christened the 2CV6] actually *participates* in the real world. And does it ever participate! You feel everything it does ... The 2CV does have grip, despite the skinny 125-15 tyres, but if you really push it, the understeer kills much of the speed you've generated. The tendency is to take corners flat-out and hang on.

Acceleration couldn't be simpler: You just keep your foot to the floor to each redline (marked at 40, 75 and 100kph on the speedometer) all the time. This soon becomes normal, and except for developing the habit (well-known to owners of early VWs) of finding ways around traffic rather than being balked without effort (especially as many of them have slowed to have a look at you). It's possible to cruise at 65mph, if the highways are essentially without gradient, and we saw an indicated 120kph (75mph) several times. The factory quotes 115kph (just under 72mph) and we'll accept this as its flat-highway, no-wind capability. Foot to the floor fuel consumption averaged 42.5mpg for the 455 miles we drove, but well over 50 should be attainable in level 55mph cruising.

Eoin Young in the *Autocar* of September 1988 compared the 2CV with the Morris Minor, both of which appeared in 1948:

The 2CV was originally powered by a four-stroke, horizontally-opposed flat twin cylinder unit of 375cc. Air cooled with a single carburettor it produced a 'startling' 9bhp at 3,500rpm.

Despite all the updating since, the spirit has been wonderfully maintained. How different Minor and 2CV were. Issigonis specified hard seats; the Citroën had sink-into armchairs which, complemented by the suspension, made for a ride of incredible comfort. The Citroën improved creature comforts still further by diverting hot air from the air-cooled engine into the cab, if required. It was several years before a heater was offered on the Morris Minor.

*The Autocar* road test of the Bijou in February 1961 gave its customary reserved but thorough opinion of its driving capabilities:

When cornering, resistance to roll is low with this suspension, so that quite large angles are reached. Nevertheless it can be cornered fast when required, although

*The 2CV celebrated its 40th anniversary in 1988.*

accompanied by considerable tyre squeal, but the car remains very stable provided that the throttle is held open. In such cornering it understeers fairly strongly – a characteristic of front drive cars – and if the throttle is then closed it steers more tightly into the corner, unless a correction is made at the steering wheel. Tyre adhesion is very good indeed on wet or dry roads.

Constant velocity joints are now fitted at the outboard ends of the drive shafts to the wheels, and these have improved greatly the smoothness of the drive on sharp corners. A little unevenness, felt at the steering wheel, remains during hard cornering.

As to the new bodywork *The Autocar* went on to say:

*The Ami's wacky shape was complemented by very usable boot space.*

A glass fibre body of British design and manufacture has transformed the appearance completely, making it acceptable in British eyes, although the tail-up attitude, when unladen, remains. In this form it is a two seater saloon with a rear seat for children; alternatively, it would be possible for an adult, sitting across the car, to use this seat for short journeys only. This better-equipped body weighs nearly 2cwt more than the standard one ... Gone is the starkness of the 2CV saloon. The interior is fully trimmed and there is a conventional instrument panel placed high on the facia.

Altogether the Bijou is a very practical car, easy to maintain and cheap to run. It provides relaxed motoring in outstanding comfort, against which must be set the relatively high noise level of its little two-cylinder engine. Although its powers of acceleration are low, it will cruise briskly on long open road runs and offers an altogether different, leisurely style of motoring which some find very appealing.

The *Automobile Engineer* of December 1960 remarked on the Bijou's performance:

Before deliveries commenced, the Bijou was subjected to unusually rigorous tests for a vehicle of this class. One of the most severe trials entailed prolonged driving at speed over the MIRA test pavé. On this destructive stretch of road it was possible for a passenger to read a newspaper while travelling at 30mph. More important, the body proved its ability to withstand this harsh treatment.

(Left and below) *Belgian 2CVs were quite different from French. Note the shape of rear window, trim strips and wing-mounted lamps.*

On poor road surfaces there is little noise inside the body from either road rumble or suspension movement. This is largely attributable to the sound deadening and non-resonant properties of the reinforced plastics body. The performance and economy of the new car are superior to those of the original 2CV model, due to the exceptionally low drag coefficient of the body form. Approximate figures for top speed and petrol consumption are 55mph and up to 60mpg respectively. The consumption rate quoted was attained during full throttle runs on the M1 motorway.

Although the new car is not intended to match the speed of popular family cars, it is quite capable of maintaining its place in a main road traffic stream. Its reliability, economy, comfortable ride, off-the-road performance, full equipment of good quality and simple maintenance make it an attractive and practical vehicle for its intended purpose. It is unusual in being specifically designed, from its inception, to withstand storage in the open, exposed to the elements.

*Another Belgian 2CV with the boot-mounted number plate and lamp.*

## EXPEDITION USE

Early expeditions in the 2CV were chronicled in the following charming contemporary reports:

On 8 May 1953, Jacques Cornet and Henri Lochon, two young French cameramen, left the pavement in front of Notre-Dame de Paris with the 2CV that had just been delivered to them. Over a year elapsed before they were to see France again, after driving over 32,300 miles, 10,560 of which were on dirt tracks.

With the smallest car in the world they had gone through the longest trip ever accomplished by an automobile. They had crossed North America from Quebec to San Francisco, Central America, South America along its longest dimension from Ecuador to Tierra del Fuego, reached the farthest austral latitude (south of the Straits of Magellan, 620 miles from the South Pole) and the highest altitude ever reached by a motor vehicle (17,782ft at the Bolivian summit of Chacaltaya).

With what better proof of sturdiness could be credited a car that went through such a trip – across seven deserts and twenty-eight countries, over countless mountain passes and forded sixty-five rivers, retaining among all these obstacles its matchless qualities? Is not this expedition the most conclusive of tests that a motor car could undergo?

The 2CV has amazed the three Americas. In each town they went through they met with a triumphant welcome. In New York their way was blocked by three thousand interested enthusiasts. In Santiago, Chile, they had an escort of ten motorcycles and thirty-five Citroën front-wheel drive cars.

But the really adventurous part began in the desert, the lonely mountains, the impenetrable bush that had to be cut through with axes, the empty wild spaces. On the way from Mexico into Guatemala the 2CV had to wade, window deep in mud, in the Tierra del Fuego it forded rivers like an amphibious, off-the-road vehicle. Of course this was not all roses: the drivers had to use patience, ingenuity, boldness.

Once while crossing a river, the car went down so deep that both carburettor and engine were flooded; thanks to the battery that had remained above water and the starter that worked under water the team were able to get to the shore by themselves, and, an hour later, to start once more.

On 12 July 1952 a Citroën 2CV was leaving Paris. Five weeks later, its two drivers M. Bernier and Dr Huguier returned to Paris having toured around the perimeter of the Mediterranean.

Result of the trip: 8,443 miles on the worst roads and dirt tracks of three continents, 21 frontiers, 112 customs. The most hazardous stage was the crossing of Egypt where the political troubles were at a high. The longest stage was 808 miles all at a stretch in the Libyan Desert from Benghasi to Bengardane. The journey was made in the best conditions without any serious incidents, without engine troubles and with perfect comfort. During cold nights, the heating system of the car provided passengers with an appreciated warmth and during the hot days in the desert they enjoyed badly needed ventilation.

The following year, with another travelling companion, Mr Duvey, Jacques Bernier started from Cape Town in his 2CV across the whole of Africa from South to North: 10,874 miles, 2,175 of them over very bad 'corrugated iron', and 1,864 in deserts, replacing only one spark plug and one headlamp bulb.

On arriving at Algiers, as the car was running fine, Bernier and Duvey suddenly decided take part in the Monte Carlo Rally. They went to Oslo to start and drove all the way Oslo–Monte Carlo–Paris.

*Jacques Seguela and J.C. Boudet drove this 2CV around the world in 1958–9.*

The sixth Tour de Belgique, organized by the Royal Automobile Club of Liège, ranks honorably among international automobile competitions.

The test consisted of a 777-mile (1,250km) drive from Liège to Spa, along a difficult route, to be covered at a compulsory average speed of 31–37mph, checking in at seventy-two control points spaced out over the route in Belgium and Luxembourg. The route proved to be particularly ticklish in the Ardennes, where one had to drive, by night, on winding mountain paths.

All sporting men who knew about this trial were unanimous in saying that it would be very rash for a 425cc 2CV to line up with much more powerful competitors.

On arriving the 2CV was five minutes ahead of its ideal schedule. Those who, at the start, had sneered at the ambition of the 2CV, just had to admit how surprised they were.

The strictly standard 2CV had brilliantly succeeded in this hard test at a speed of 33.9mph, including the seventy-two stops for checking and the four for refuelling. It was the first time that a car under 500cc had completed the Tour de Belgique.

The 2CV got first rank among cars under 500cc and drivers Hanlet and Paquay were rewarded with a splendid cup offered by the City of Luxembourg. Such is the official victory of an AZ425 whose sporting career will no doubt be full of glory.

Running for three consecutive days and nights on icy roads, in the Scandinavian snow and fog, with the thermometer between +5°F and −40°F is rather an unusual feat for a normally-built automobile. On the drivers' part it requires considerable tenacity, and from the machine, a resistance above the average.

Yet it is as severe a test as this that four 2CV 425cc Citroën cars have faced. The circuit was run under the control of the Automobile Club-Royal which had arranged for twelve timing checks over the 2,640 miles of this Tour de Suede. Having started from Stockholm on Thursday 3 February 1955 at 10am the four cars came back to their starting point on Sunday evening. They had run for seventy-eight consecutive hours.

The average speed actually obtained was 33.54mph, the first two cars arriving together on Sunday at 4.05pm, the third twenty-five minutes later. The fourth car alone was delayed by ninety minutes after the preceding one, owing to a mistake in the route.

Most of the time the cars ran by night; we should not forget that, in a northern winter, the sun is visible only for six hours daily. Besides, weather conditions had been disastrous and just such as might discourage the hardiest enthusiasts: mist, fog, snow, sleet; as though in sport, nature had piled up difficulties. In the south, the drivers, following one another at ten minutes intervals, could only find their way by watching for the yellow line marking the middle of the road. In the north, as it was impossible to read the road signs, some drivers went astray. Huge reindeer herds considerably hindered the progress of the cars.

The mechanical behaviour of the 2CV was perfect all through the race: not the slightest mechanical trouble, not even one plug to change. The engines ran continuously, even during stops (except while refuelling).

As for the fuel consumption, it was not over 43.5mpg.

The 2CV has thus shown once more how adaptable to weather conditions and road difficulties the automobile is. Among torrid desert sands as well as in the snow storms of the Great North, the 2CV behaves very well indeed.

## Comparative cars of the period

### Renault 4CV

The 4CV Renault was to beat the 2CV Citroën into production by several months and the Renault stand featuring the 4CV was alongside Boulanger's new baby Citroën at the 1948 Paris Motor Show. With a much more complicated body style, the 4CV was a curved rounded peanut of a car with definite charm. The 4CV was also the first Renault to reach the million-produced mark. A simple three-speed gearbox was used via a classic little 'marble on top of a knitting needle' gear lever and the rear-mounted, four-cylinder, water-cooled 747cc engine gave out around 20bhp. Later engines, like the Dauphine, were 850cc and could double the output to 40bhp. Cruising speed was around the 50mph mark and the 4CV – weighing only 600kg – could return 40mpg. Its coil spring suspension was stiff but the car stuck to the road well and a similar driving gait to that of the 2CV was adopted: that of maintaining momentum at nearly all costs.

Sturdily made in heavy-gauge steel, the 4CV survived well and there are many on the road today. Most are saloons but there are some roll-top versions with a fabric roof rolled back á la 2CV.

A rear-wheel drive car with a version of the swing axle suspension as fitted to the Volkswagen Beetle, and probably more controversially to the 300SL Mercedes-Benz, the 4CV is said to have nervous handling, but like any of these things it is all relative and a design that gave enthusiastic drivers heart-stopping moments, like the Mercedes-Benz set-up in its powerful 300SL sports car, could be quite acceptable in a small family saloon of just a few horsepower. Rear-engined cars have to be driven differently – you can't invoke a rear wheel slide in the wet and expect to correct it with ease.

By the time the Citroën 2CV appeared on the stand of the 1948 Paris Motor Show the 4CV Renault was being produced at the rate of 300 a day and by 1950 the figure had increased to the yearly total of 120,000. While the 4CV beat the

*The Renault 4CV, 1955.*

2CV into production and was a million-seller by 1960, it was comparatively short-lived, surviving only until 1961. The 2CV leapt ahead of it and was soon surpassing the million mark itself.

## Renault 4

Lack of passenger and luggage space and the bad reputation given by its suspension persuaded Renault to drop the 4CV and create its replacement with inspiration from Citroën itself: a platform chassis bearing a light body of simple, unstressed panels with a front-mounted engine and front-wheel drive. The soft suspension had plenty of travel – like the 2CV – and passengers were seated well within the wheelbase. The engine was more traditional than the Citroën's: it was a four-cylinder water-cooled unit of 747cc, giving 24bhp. Arranged very much like that of the Traction Avant, the Renault 4 gearbox was mounted ahead of the engine and

was operated by a long lever which extended across the top of the engine and protruded through a hole in the dashboard, also emulating the 2CV. Other similarities include rack-and-pinion steering and, again like the Traction Avant, torsion bar suspension front and rear.

While the 4 could be accused of being a Renault version of the 2CV it had many innovative features of its own. The true hatchback configuration gave it plenty of space and with the rear seats folded flat it was easily turned into a van. It had a sealed engine cooling system designed to be trouble-free and make the car as usable in extreme ranges of temperatures as was the 2CV.

The Renault 4 was built in massive numbers too, almost surpassing the 2CV's total. More than eight million 4s were built between 1961 and 1992 and it was subject to many improvements and changes. Like the 2CV it was built all around the world, the last car being made at the last surviving factory in Yugoslavia.

*The Renault 4, 1963.*

## Volkswagen Beetle

The Volkswagen Beetle shared the same design brief with the 2CV: to mobilize the masses in a cheap and affordable manner. But in background and mechanical design they couldn't be more different. It was during the mid-1930s that Adolf Hitler awarded to Ferdinand Porsche the contract to produce the 'People's Car' or 'Strength through Joy' car. Hans Ledwinka of Tatra comes into the story, as his design for a bubble-shaped rear-engined car with rear engine louvres had been made into a prototype before Porsche was given the Nazi contract. The Tatra prototype design was 'borrowed' by Porsche with the full backing of Hitler's regime. A copyright infringement suit was filed by Tatra but it was, of course, ignored. After the war Tatra filed successfully, winning damages. To look at photographs of the Tatra prototype and then the early Volkswagen prototype is to look at much the same car.

Not so much a copy as a closely allied design, the Volkswagen did not appear as prototype until 1936, and nearly complete production prototypes appeared in 1938. It was much the same story as Citroën at that time with its Toute Petit Voiture. As was the case with all civilian motor car production, wartime halted development as factories were put over to producing the instruments of war. No Volkswagens were ever bought under the Nazi regime.

After the conflict it was the occupying British and American forces which put the Volkswagen into production. It went on to become a runaway success like the 2CV, but the Beetle is still made in Mexico today and over the years it has surpassed the 2CV many times over in terms of production figures: more than twenty-two million have been made.

While the two cars' ultimate markets may have been similar, their construction is very different. The Volkswagen is much heavier and has a larger engine, but its top speed is only a little higher. It fared worse on fuel consumption, too. The 2CV's superior power-to-weight ratio gives it the edge of frugality and performance and the design itself is much simpler. The Volkswagen's body panels are of complicated double curves and each panel would require a series of expensive press tools to produce. There is more sophistication in the Volkswagen as the door sealing was designed to be watertight – at least for a few minutes. Try driving a 2CV into a pond and you will discover how different the 2CV doors are!

*A 1950 Volkswagen Beetle.*

For practicality of purpose the 2CV wins hands down but the Volkswagen Beetle went on to become the most popular car of all time, if production figures are anything to go by.

## Panhard Dyna/PL17

The first Dyna Panhard, the Dyna X, was introduced in 1946 to an original design by Jean-Albert Grégoire. The Dyna name was probably an extraction from the 1937 Dynamique. Like Citroën, Panhard was experimenting with weight-saving construction methods and had years of experience using lightweight alloys. Cast aluminium crankcases were made by them before 1914, and in 1924 the 16CV sports model had cylinder and crankcase castings in Alpax. In 1922 Panhard sponsored a sports body manufactured from aluminium castings by Montupet and assembled by Ansart Audineau. The contemporary success of the Weymann fabric coachwork meant that the alloy venture didn't continue. From being a leading maker in the early years of motoring, Panhard made only light cars after World War Two. Its designs for flat, horizontally-opposed engines were very successful. A strange-looking flat-12 Panhard engine was used in tanks for many years and progress was being made with a flat four.

Citroën had a share in Panhard from 1955 and when the Dyna range of effective if strange cars began to expand, Citroën found itself up against a worthy competitor. The elegant 24CT and 24BT models of 1964–67 were produced against Citroën's wishes and by 1965 Citroën bought Panhard outright as it didn't want a direct competitor in this area of the market. It put disc brakes on all the latest 24CT/BT models as a parting gift but stopped all production of Panhards in 1967. So ended the run of France's oldest car manufacturer, having been involved in motor cars since 1889. The last model, with an 850cc engine, was capable of better than 100mph. Streamlining and good power-to-weight ratio counts for a lot.

The aluminium body of the Dyna and PL17 was built on a cast aluminium frame and clad in aluminium panels. Grégoire wanted the chassis to be aluminium too, but it is likely he couldn't get the strength required without making the chassis inordinately bulky. Steel was used instead. The whole car weighed just 1,332lb and with its small 610cc flat twin engine was capable of 70–75mph.

*The 1950 Panhard Dyna 120 saloon.*

A jumble of strange shapes is the dominating impression on first seeing the post-war Panhard. The panel's startling swirls and curves are quite unlike anything else. Yet the car's styling works. It wouldn't if the details weren't similarly idiosyncratic. It's rather like a Lutyens house where all the doors, handles, windows and even light fittings are designed with the whole thing in mind. The Panhard is like that with neatly original fittings everywhere, including neat window winders working in a dainty arc on the door trims and the teardrop-shaped petrol filler completing the Art Deco styling on the rear wing.

The flat twin engine – also air-cooled – is interesting both technically and visually. The entire front of the car hinges up alligator fashion and the bonnet is sealed against the wheel arches when closed, to prevent road dirt from entering. The spare wheel is mounted atop the engine with the air-cleaner protruding through it. The wheels themselves have a large central hole which effectively bolts around the edge of the drum brakes. Twin exhaust pipes emanate from the cooling fan housing – a work of crafted aluminium art – and run dangerously close to the metalastic engine mountings. Local heat here can be the cause of mounting failure. Valvegear is particularly unusual: a single torsion bar spring operates both inlet and exhaust valves. The two-cylinder engine of the PL17 displaces just 848cc yet puts out 60bhp. This will propel the 12.5cwt Panhard to 90mph plus. The curious but robust valvegear allied to double roller crankshaft bearings allows revving beyond 6,500rpm.

The all-alloy engine seems to work best in the 3,000–6,000rpm range and, like the 2CV, the Panhard encourages an interesting driving compromise between safety and expediency: to maintain progress you really have to keep it wound up using all available power. In the absence of synchromesh, first to second changes are time consuming and revs have to die away to almost nothing before silent changes can be made. The engine seems happiest under full throttle and once you've accepted this rather brutish method of progress with a feeling approaching calm, the Panhard drives rather well. You begin to accept the body roll and squealing tyres as charming rather than life-threatening and this mode of car travel can grow on you. It goes even better if you wear a beret and smoke Caporals.

Steering is rack-and-pinion, like the 2CV, but the front suspension is by double transverse leaf springs which form the upper and lower wishbones. Short driveshafts with constant-velocity joints are placed between the springs. At the rear a V-shaped axle pivots on a rubber bush at the centre of the crossmember and trailing arms connect to triple torsion bars running transversely along the same crossmember. Telescopic dampers control movement front and rear.

The PL17 was launched in 1959 with some spectacular colour schemes including a light and dark two-tone lilac. Bodywork was essentially like the previous Dyna Z model but without that model's 'cyclops' lamp at the front and with revised front and rear treatment, featuring streamlined lamp clusters and a hooded extension to the roof over the rear screen.

Interiors sported a fantastically futuristic dashboard plastic pod surrounding the steering column and looking for all the world like the cockpit of a Dan Dare spaceship. The gloveboxes were particularly striking, being long opening cylinders arranged along the dashboard. Details are well designed, but quirky, too much so for some buyers. Rear-hinged 'suicide' doors remained until 1960 when French laws changed, and right-hand drive cars became available shortly after. Michelin tyres were a standard fitting.

Many variants appeared, including estates, vans and a beautiful cabriolet. Bodies were restyled in 1963 featuring less aluminium trim and exposed, finned brake drums which have since been fitted to earlier models. Carrying capacity is increased by removing the rear seat, thus exposing an unobstructed floorspace extending to the rear of the front seats. Bench seats at the front were dropped in favour of reclining 'Relmax' individual seats. Cars so fitted sported a Relmax script on the rear wings. Later the model became known as 17B or 17BT for Berline or Berline Tigre to fit in with the new model 24CT (Coupé/Tigre) introduced in 1964. Production of the 17BT ceased in 1965 after 130,000 had been made.

## Morris Minor

The Morris Minor began to roll off the production lines in September 1948 and was not hailed with universal approval as the successor to the Morris Eight. It is said that Morris's owner, Lord Nuffield, didn't speak to designer Alec Issigonis until 1960, when the millionth Minor was produced.

Turkish-born Issigonis was not the run-of-the-mill designer. He didn't have the thought that 'Britishness' must prevail in car design and there are many foreign influences on his designs, including, for the Minor, the 1941 Packard. The design exercise was to fit four people into a car with minimum external size. That the result was perhaps too cramped inside can be seen in the 4in-wide raised strip running down the bonnet line. The prototype was chopped down the middle and the extra strip lapped in. That strip was to remain as testament to the move right up to the last Minor. Issigonis had wanted to put a flat-four engine of his own design into the Minor, but there were problems and the engine which was to make it into the 1948 car was the 918cc engine first used by Morris in 1934.

However, engine aside, the Minor was innovative in its way. Torsion bar suspension was complemented by rack-and-pinion steering, the whole being encased in a monocoque construction. Interior appointments were spartan: the seats were very firm and, unlike the 2CV, there was no standard heater. As Issigonis said, 'Make the seats hard, keep the driver uncomfortable and he'll concentrate. What do they want a heater for? They can wear an overcoat.' The Minor had quite a roomy boot for its day and housed the spare wheel in another tray under the boot floor, thus avoiding the necessity of removing all the luggage to gain access to it.

As Issigonis wanted smaller than average wheels, so as to reduce unsprung weight on his torsion bar suspension, Dunlop was approached and provided the unusual size tyres. Later it was to help Issigonis with his next design, the Mini with its even smaller wheels. Issigonis claims to have designed the Minor in all its details, down to handles and knobs, and the same was true of the Mini a little later.

But perhaps unusual transatlantic styling did find buyers, and the Minor was soon to enter the British way of life and become a success. The

*A 1949 Morris Minor.*

millionth Minor was made in 1960 and the following year Morris was to make Minor Millions, 350 of them finished in lilac and with the usual 1000 chrome badge re-made to read 1000000. The Morris Minor became an institution and was made in many different forms. Convertibles, the wood-trimmed Traveller (also known, at least by Dame Edna Everidge as a 'dinky little half-timbered car.'), vans, pickups and the odd-looking Post Office van fitted with rubber wings (those Post Office drivers ...).

The suspension was to be much praised in the motoring press. The Autocar's S.C.H. Davis was to describe it as, '... one of the best in my experience, while the car handles beautifully on corners. The engine may be small but it is exceedingly willing and will pull right down to the bitter end even if you do not, as you should, use the gears for the purpose they are intended.'

The important thing about both the Minor and the 2CV was that each had the difficult to define quality that made them charming and attractive. The only way it can best be described is that a tiny child in a pram will point at a Morris Minor or a Citroën 2CV and recognize it as having a happy 'face'. The same could not be said of most cars today.

## The 2CV according to Citroën

This Citroën press release appeared sometime in 1957:

### The 2CV Citroën

The striking impression created throughout the world when the DS19 was presented at the

*1963 Fourgonnette in typical pose.*

French Motor Show in 1955 as the car of the future presented to the public today, has apparently cast a shadow on another element of the Citroën production: the 2CV.

Yet this vehicle, seemingly less sensational than its big sister, has won over thousands of users and despite an unceasingly growing production, French users of the 2CV wait for it three or four years. Such is the success it has gained amongst all publics.

After all, it is a vehicle utilizable both in towns and in the country, it can carry passengers just as it can transport materials sometimes very cumbersome.

Like the DS, the 2CV is worthy of the Citroën Works' reputation for reliability and quality, for technical ingenuity and prowess is soundly established.

### Appearance of the 2CV

In 1936, Citroën had begun study of a popular car of small cylinder-volume. At that time, the forms of the prototype foreshadowed the present line. In the mind of the Directors of the firm the 2CV was intended for rural customers but after the war, city-dwellers proved that the vehicle could be successfully adapted to all classes of users.

At the 1948 Show, Citroën presented the 2CV to the public. (Due to circumstances, research was abandoned during the war but work was resumed at the end of hostilities.)

The appearance of the 2CV caused surprise and astonishment; numerous were those who decided they found it ugly, but soon, blind to the appearance they discovered its immense services. If its form astonishes, the ability of its design raises enthusiasm. It very rapidly became the first of the world's small cars. There are four roomy places, its extremely economic engine makes 70.60 to 56.40 statute miles per imperial gallon (it consumes 4–5 litres × 100km). It is light and will not wear out. The air-cooled drive is in front, its spare parts are moderate in cost, its excellent springing improves road-behaviour, economizes mechanisms and avoids fatigue.

This suspension is composed of an inertia-beater; a mobile mass enclosed in a case moving to and fro, resists the jumping of the road. In addition the suspension arms are connected in pairs longitudinally to avoid rolling. The seats are of the 'transatlantic' type with rubber straps. They are detachable either to make room in the rear for bulky elements or use as chairs outside the vehicle etc.

## Levallois, kingdom of the 2CV

It is in one of the thirty-two French Citroën works, at Levallois, a Paris suburb, that the 2CV is assembled. In this modern factory numerous operations are automatic.

To save space and time, transport of complete elements of a vehicle is made on balancelles on an overhead conveyor.

Each component of a 2CV is machined and assembled in a particular workshop: engines, axle cranks, suspension pots, floorings and bodies, spare parts.

When those elements are finished, they are hooked to *balancelles* hanging from the overhead carousel which is several kilometres long and moves round without a stop.

At the beginning of their course, balancelles are progressively loaded; their path is along the assembly line where each worker takes the part to be put on the vehicle passing in front of him.

Throughout the operations, whether machining or assembling, multiple controls check the work. At the end of the line, a last super-control turns down without pity cars not satisfying certain criterions of quality and working, established by carefully perfected tests.

The most spectacular realizations in the Levallois works are undoubtedly the multiple-spot automatic welding machines, in particular the one used for chassis preparations automatically receiving 360 welding spots in less than one minute.

Another spectacular realization is the automatic bonderization and painting tunnel. It comprises a gigantic chain of saw teeth into which the 2CV cars enter, hanging in pairs, to pass through first a bonderization vat, then a furnace, another vat for painting and priming, another furnace etc ... in all eleven protection operations. This device is two storeys high and several hundred metres long. Speed of the overhead line is calculated so that all the operations have time to take place without the chain ever having to stop. Of course, all those operations take place without interventions by man except at the control apparatus.

## An unprecedented success

Customers very rapidly rushed at the 2CV because it lends itself to practically all uses on any ground and in any country whatever.

For instance, it is used by Scandinavian Automobile Clubs as breakdown cars on icy roads in the polar circle.

It is also used by the Administration and Post Offices of reclaimed dykes in Holland because it is the only vehicle able to cross the dykes recently reclaimed from the sea, the soil of which is still spongy.

Again, it has become the choice of the Maharajah Kumar of Sikken who renounced buying a foreign limousine to buy a 2CV, particularly adapted for use in a country of high altitude like the Sikkin (3,300m high in the Himalaya chain, in a severe climate, with primitive roads periodically damaged by the River Tista and where petrol is extremely rare).

It also very rapidly became the most important part of the perfect explorer's equipment: more than twenty exploration trips, ethnological or archeological journeys across the world have consecrated its success. Amongst them can be indicated the linking of Canada and Land of Fire, realized from 8 May 1953 to 10 May 1954, by Jacques Cornet and Henry Lochon who covered 32,000 miles (51,200km) with a 375cc Citroën 2CV, beating the automobile altitude record of 17,716ft (5,429m, Mount Chacaltaya), the austral automobile record (Land of Fire) crossing twenty-three countries, seven deserts (amongst which the redoubtable desert of Atacava, 1,739 miles), crossed sixty-five rivers by fording, made the first Mexico–Guatemala connection by covering 149 miles (240km) through jungle cutting their way through with a machete covering 807 miles (1,300km) in the Land of Fire.

More recently (from 2 August 1956 to 27 April 1957) Jacques Cornet again used a 2CV for making the trip Paris–Tokyo–Paris with Georges Kihm. They crossed twenty-nine countries, covered 27,961 miles (45,000km) and in that way, Jacques Cornet went round the world in a 2CV; 62,137 miles (100,000km). Their route was Paris–Venice–Salonica–Athens–Istanbul–Ispahan–Caspian–Kabul–Pakistan–Lahore–New Delhi–Calcutta–Singapore–Bangkok–Pnom Penh–Saigon–Hong Kong–Yokohama–Tokyo–Hiroshima–Kyn Shin.

We mention too the expedition of Erik de Waubert and Henry Lochon crossing 12,427 miles (20,000km) in the Mexican jungle amongst Tarahumaras Indians, a troglodyte race descending from Aztecs; also the communication Paris–Tibet by R.J. Godet and M. Batique during which the 2CV crossed six passes higher than 9,000ft.

### The world vocation of the 2CV

Thus it is proved that the 2CV is capable of satisfying all acquirers in any region of the world and rapidly, orders came in from abroad.

That is why Citroën has decided to increase export possibilities by establishing in various countries, assembly lines for the 2CV. At present there is one in Slough in England, at Forest in Belgium, since this year, 1957, in the free zone in Spain at Vigo, and at the Cambodge.

Establishment of assembly lines leads to:

- reduction of transport expenses
- use of local products for non-mechanical parts (especially textiles)
- use of local labour

... making available, in the country where there is an assembly line for vehicles which are the least expensive in the world and offer greater services than other types of car.

The advantage of establishing a 2CV assembly line in certain foreign countries is so evident that it was immediately understood by the Spanish Government which takes an interest therein also by the Cambodge Government for the most recent Citroën assembly line: that of Pnom Penh in the Cambodge.

For Spain as for Cambodge, a vehicle of this type at once proved a vehicle adapted to the country, its roads and tracks.

Experiments, confirmed by experience, have shown that in large and small agricultural areas, the vehicles gave the same services as much heavier cars and that finally their cost price per km is lower by 50 per cent than any other means of transport.

Moreover it is the ideal vehicle on the economic plans as it is cheaper for purchase and upkeep, therefore extremely interesting for foreign currency treasuries of Governments.

In the Cambodge in particular, the success of the 2CV van (551lb; 250kg) is such that whereas assembling has not yet begun, the Company has already booked 3,000 firm orders.

The year 1958 should allow the assembling company in the Cambodge to increase its rhythms, reduce cost price and use local resources to a maximum.

### Assembly lines outside France

2CVs intended for export are fitted with a special equipment the works call 'P.O.', consisting of an oil-bath air-filter, chassis reinforcement, reinforced bumpers, specially in front where they are in the form of a spatula of a ski to attack sand-dunes more easily.

2CVs for assembling outside France are shipped from Paris, to Slough, to Forest, to Vigo, and Pnom Penh. The elements are carefully wrapped and stowed in special cases for despatch by rail, and steamer towards their assembly lines. The cases are unpacked, contents checked then assembled with care by local labour.

# 8 Racing 2CVs

Although the Citroën 2CV looks about as suitable for racing as a shopping trolley, it has in fact been involved in motorsport for many years. In the 1960s Citroën organized Rally 'Raids': endurance races over thousands of miles and across continents which were keenly contested by sometimes hundreds of 2CVs and derivatives. Then in the 1970s came 2CV Cross – off-road racing for 2CVs – once again organized by Citroën, and attended by thousands of enthusiastic spectators throughout Europe.

2CV circuit racing began in Britain in 1989 under the auspices of the 2CV Club of Great Britain. The first meeting was held at Mallory Park with a very respectable grid of

*Even with comparatively little power the racing 2CVs can still kick up the dust.*

twenty-two cars and was won by Royce Grey, the current chairman. It won instant recognition as close, exciting, affordable sport and these are still the main attractions of 2CV racing.

In 1990 the first 24-hour 2CV race was held at Mondello Park, near Dublin. The success of this venture exceeded all expectations and the annual trek to Ireland is now a standard item on the Championship agenda. In fact, most people seem to know Mondello Park as 'that circuit where they hold the 24-hour 2CV race!'

Nine years on the racing is still just as popular as ever with both competitors and spectators. After Ian Flux, of Touring Car

fame, raced a 2CV in the Pembrey One Hour Race he is reported by *Autosport* to have said, 'The Touring Car Championship would kill for racing like this.'

It really is that good! In some ways the relatively slow speed of the 2CV is a bonus in that it makes the racing closer. Drivers regularly take corners two, three- or even four-abreast, and then slipstream the car in front before trying to overtake before the next bend! Of course the car behind is trying to do the same so the next corner will probably be taken three- or four-abreast as well.

2CV racing regularly receives excellent reviews in the motoring press and is very popular with spectators and marshals alike.

*2CVs stream past the start line in the 24-hour endurance race at Mondello Park, Dublin.*

*It is unusual to see only two 2CVs on a corner.*

Over the last two years efforts have been made to reduce 'race incidents', generally successfully, so that while the racing is fiercely competitive it is also relatively clean and good natured. Even those drivers further down the field are dicing throughout the race, and often the best action is in the middle of the field, so nobody is left out! On many occasions the qualifying results have been so close that as many as seven or eight cars are separated on the grid by just one second.

One of the great advantages of 2CV racing is the good availability of cheap donor cars, the abundance of spares, and the relatively small amount of modification required to transform the road-going version into a

race-winning car. Being a basic and simple vehicle, the whole process of conversion into a racing car is reasonably straightforward and you do not need to be a mechanical genius to build a racing 2CV.

Over the years there have been some changes to the technical regulations which have meant that more mechanical parts of the car can be modified. Many of these modifications have been made for reasons of safety, whilst the rest are for better handling or performance. In general the modifications require only basic tools and knowledge, such as removing the choke flap from the carburettor or lengthening the gear lever. Other modifications require welding or the use of

*Lowered suspension helps the handling of the 2CV.*

other less common equipment, such as altering the springs in the suspension cylinders or modifying the front suspension arms. In these cases the financial outlay is still negligible, and in most cases there are members of the club who can do these modifications for you for a small charge if you do not have the facilities available yourself. Alternatively, there are always good 2CVs around which have already been prepared and raced. Buying one of these can often be cheaper than building your own and of course it takes away the hard work.

For several years the Championship has been sponsored by Firestone, which provides each competitor with a number of free tyres. Apart from the 24-hour race, the tyres normally last a season, so the chances are you wont be needing to buy too many tyres. The Championship has also been co-sponsored by Andyspares, which is an independent supplier of Citroën parts. Each competitor starting a race receives cash, and Andyspares is now

going to produce a special price list of parts for 2CV racing club members.

Most of the competitors have their own sponsorship, which can range from large companies offering considerable financial support to local suppliers giving free oil and parts. It is certainly worthwhile spending some time arranging sponsorship, and in many cases firms are more than willing to back someone starting in the hope that they might rise to the top and carry their initial sponsors with them. The fact that you will be competing in some Best of British Motorsport meetings, with the chances of television coverage, should carry some weight and it is certainly worth mentioning. It is also worth mentioning that the club, through various initiatives, will be supporting selected charities throughout the season.

The 2CV Championship comprises ten rounds on circuits throughout Britain and also the 24-hour race in Ireland. These meetings are held at circuits such as Brands

*Close encounter combat typical of 2CV racing.*

Hatch, Donington Park, Silverstone and Oulton Park, on weekends between April and October. Being a part of the Best of British Motorsport package means being involved in prestigious, televised events together with the likes of Formula 3, TVR Tuscans and Rover Turbos. At Brands Hatch the club generally supports the Trucks and at Silverstone the Mondeo Eurocars.

All new racing members of the club will be assigned an 'uncle' or 'buddy' who is an accomplished member to help and guide him or her through the pitfalls of starting up, from technical advice on preparing the car to where to sign on at the first race. The club believes that this is a great help and alleviates any worries that new members may have about being left out in the cold once they have signed up.

## THE MONDELLO PARK 24-HOURS ENDURANCE RACE

The highlight of the 2CV racing calendar is the Mondello Park 24-Hour Race. This is an attraction few other forms of motorsport can boast of and it provides all the drama and excitement of Le Mans. Mondello Park is a tight and twisty circuit in the Republic of Ireland, close to Dublin. The race was conceived by the Irish Motor Racing Club's Simon North and Competition Director David Byers. The circuit itself has everything needed to make a perfect 2CV race, with a blend of hairpins, double apex corners, left-handers and a straight long enough to read your pitboard and take a short but welcome breather! In most years there is also a reasonable dose of Irish rain

*A mass of 2CVs jostle for position on the corners at Mondello Park.*

*Pit stops for driver changes in the 24-hour endurance race at Mondello Park.*

to add to the excitement and tension. In one weekend most competitors will race in the region of 250 miles, which would take about two complete seasons in normal circumstances. Add to that the exciting atmosphere and the Guinness, and you could end up with a perfect and memorable weekend.

First timers to 2CV racing are amazed to find out how much fun it is to race such a slow car. Most of the rules of motor racing are thrown out of the window as it dawns on you that the braking point at corners is far, far later than you could ever imagine. Maintaining progress is the name of the game and with such limited bhp under your foot, any mistakes at corners can scrub off valuable speed which takes ages to regain. Let the front or rear slide and you've lost several seconds and some very cherished mph in the process. Get a corner right with late braking and jamming the gear lever into third, and the apparently suicidal conduct turns into a moan from the driver as the 2CV incongruously traverses the corner with almost no tyre squeal: 'So that's how you're supposed to do it …'.

Writer Phil Llewellin was impressed enough with the event to write the following report published in the *Daily Telegraph* in August 1998 under the title 'Charge of the Lightweight Brigade'.

In days of yore, dauntless knights clad themselves in suits of armour and sallied forth astride mighty warhorses, seeking anything from the Holy Grail to damsels in distress. Fast forward to 1998 and we find Sir Aubrey Brocklebank donning fireproof overalls and adjusting his glasses before charging into battle aboard nothing more mettlesome or beautifully caparisoned than one of Citroën's famously idiosyncratic 'tin snails'.

A keen competitor in Vintage Sports Car Club events, generally at the wheel of his pre-war Lagonda Rapier, 'Strawberry Throttlecrank' was at Mondello Park, a few miles west of Dublin, for Ireland's answer to Le Mans.

Races in general, and 24 hour races in particular, were not what Citroën had in mind when the 2CV was launched in 1948.

*Flat out on the straight, 2CVs are very closely matched.*

Conceived before the war, the quintessentially bucolic and utilitarian Deux Chevaux was designed to provide Jean-Pierre and Marie-Louise with a very cheap, practical and simple alternative to the horse.

First run in 1989, Les Vingt-Quatre Heures du Mondello Park is the highlight of the ten-round British 2CV Championship, which involves much shorter races on such famous tracks as Silverstone and Brands Hatch. The main attractions include affordability – you can buy a reasonably competitive car for around £2500 – close racing and any amount of delightfully old-fashioned camaraderie.

Martin Woodley, the 2CV Racing Club's ebullient, indefatigable and hard driving secretary, cheerfully admits that weighing 17 stones is a disadvantage when driving a car powered by a twin-cylinder, 602cc engine. This also explains why the words 'The Fat Controller' form part of his 2CV's livery.

Citroën's baby was engineered to be driven across fields without scrambling a basket of eggs, so the standard suspension is as soft as marshmallow. This being my first experience of 2CV racing, I had visions of cars cornering like schooners in the Roaring Forties. Although the rules permit lowering and stiffening, they still adopt far more interesting angles than modern racing cars. They are also considerably faster than the common or garden 2CV in a straight line, because the best engines are tuned to deliver about 40bhp and will rev to almost 8000rpm before flinging their contents halfway across the parish.

While few drivers have nightmares about being able to handle that amount of power, it does represent an increase of about 50 per cent. Making such a highly tuned engine hold together for two complete rounds of the clock demands high standards of engineering and driving. The front-wheel drive 2CV's push-pull gear lever, which sprouts from the dashboard like an umbrella handle, makes it all too easy to select the wrong cog in the heat of the moment. This can spoil your day in less time than it takes to shout 'Merde!', but an engine is light enough to be lifted by one man and can be changed in as little as eight minutes, with the help of understanding friends who also happen to be top-notch mechanics.

The newest of Mondello Park's four circuits kept the Citroënistes alert by packing all manner of corners into 1.74 gently undulating miles. An additional challenge was posed by the new loop's surface providing significantly more grip than the old part of the track, particularly when County Kildare was hammered by heavy rain, which made the night that much more of a challenge.

Newcomers to nocturnal racing included Brocklebank, one of the four-man squad assembled by Bill Carr, a cheerful Scottish doctor who also collects old Rolls-Royces and, incidentally, used to have a house-trained pet pig called Harley, in honour of Harley-Davidson. He was hoping to do better than in 1997, when Carr Racing finished last but one in a field of 32.

At the other end of the experience scale, the team that was destined to finish second featured Mondello Park's owner, Martin Birrane, who has ten Le Mans starts to his credit.

*This car's drivers included two with a total of twenty Le Mans starts to their credit. It finished second.*

*Team leader Richard Dalton drives the car that won the race.*

*Last pit stop for the winning car.*

One of his three co-drivers, David Kennedy, has also contested the world's most famous 24-hour race ten times and drove a Formula One Shadow in 1980's World Championship. They agreed that racing a Citroën 2CV was great fun – 'Otherwise we wouldn't be here' – and just as challenging, in its own eccentric way, as hammering down the Mulsanne straight on the serious side of 200mph. Maintaining momentum is the name of the game.

The promise of old-style, wheel-to-wheel racing for lap after lap was what lured my wife and I across the Irish Sea. There was no need to pull Martin Woodley's leg about invoking the Trade Description Act, because reality exceeded expectations by a wide margin and kept reminding us that all things are relative.

Grand Prix cars look boring, more often than not, because the races tend to be high-speed processions in which overtaking is big news. Murray Walker's vocal chords would have needed replacing after the first hour at Mondello Park, because 2CV racing is all about bunches of five, six or seven jostling for position as they corner with tyres squealing like piglets that have just discovered the awful truth about pork sausages.

With so much happening, on the track and in the pits, it was easy to forget that the beautifully prepared and expertly managed ECAS 2CV Parts car of Richard Dalton, Peter Sparrow and Edward Mason was in the lead from the start, and finished seven laps ahead of Team Birrane after averaging 46.93mph.

Carr's Racing's 27th place was due to a team effort that included Lady Brocklebank's expertise with pit signals: 'I was apprehensive, but can't believe how much fun it has been, despite not having any sleep,' she said.

The fingers of one hand were sufficient to count cars that had no body damage what-soever, but only one of the starters failed to finish, due to its engine catching fire literally minutes from the flag. This being Ireland, the team's £50 consolation prize was promptly converted into Guinness.

The 24-Hour race is now held at Snetterton. For details contact the 2CV Racing Club at www.2cvracing.co.uk

## THE 2CV RACING CLUB

The 2CV Racing Club is there to help any would-be racegoers get started and it has an impressive list of events open to members. Membership is available on two levels. Racing Members have full voting rights at the Annual General Meeting, discount on club merchandise, social invitations, *Snails Pace* magazine and technical bulletins. Membership is £35. Associate Members have no vote at the AGM but get discount on club merchandise, social invitations and *Snails Pace* magazine. Membership is £10.

The racing calendar extends from April to October and includes events at Mallory Park, Anglesey, Knockhill, Mondello, Oulton Park, Lydden Hill, Cadwell Park and Pembrey. The Club's address is given in the list of addresses at the end of Chapter 9.

To race at events drivers need 2CV Racing Club Membership, BARC Membership, a RACSMA National B racing licence (which can be acquired after taking an ARDS course at a racing circuit). Cars need to be prepared to RAC Blue Book regulations with regard to roll cage, safety equipment, seats and belts. Car build regulations are available from the BARC.

Cars can be lowered by stiffening and adapting suspension cylinders; the fitting of adjustable shock absorbers is recommended. Front steering arms can be turned to remove cadence angle. Gearboxes are the

*The finish for one of the durable 2CVs.*

standard 2CV6 type. Engines can be pepped up by machining the heads to increase compression and cylinder head volumes can be increased. The club recommends Firestone tyres. Costs are a fraction of 'ordinary' racing and cars ready-prepared are available from £1,500 to £3,000 depending on performance and specifications.

## RAIDS AND RALLIES

Citroën itself used to sponsor 'Raids', which can loosely be translated as ridiculously hazardous expeditions. From the series of individuals in single cars going on massive journeys in the late 1950s and early 1960s the company decided to organize its own events to include many cars in the running. Citroën's director of public relations, Jacques Wolgensinger, organized the officially sponsored events, and apart from being a lot of fun, the events were an ideal mechanism to display the rugged 2CV at its desert-crossing, mountain-climbing best. The Raids were to echo the convoys that Citroën organized as publicity events in the 1920s and 1930s –

for instance in the Kegresse tracked Citroëns. The first of these was timed to coincide with the recent launch of the Méhari and took the form of a 9,320-mile rally from Liege to Dakar and back, starting on 6 July 1969 and returning on 3 September. Traversing as it did thousands of miles across deserts, it proved the worth of the rugged Méhari – twenty-five of which took part – and was the perfect publicity stunt.

The next year Citroën arranged an even bigger event with 494 flat-twin-engined cars taking part in the Paris to Kabul and back Raid, around 17,000km in total. Of these, 320 returned to Paris having completed the round trip within Citroën's own time limits for arrival and return.

In 1971 Citroën offered ten new cars as prizes for the Raid that year which was Paris–Persepolis–Paris. The ten new cars were awarded for the best taped commentary and photographic coverage of the expedition. More than 500 cars took part in this event which was sponsored by Total and Radio-Télé-Luxembourg.

The third mass rally organized by Citroën was the Raid Afrique of 1973 when sixty 2CVs

*Fortunately, a 2CV engine can be changed in a few minutes.*

and Dyanes – all with the later 602cc engines – were despatched from Le Havre by ship to Africa with a back-up fleet of Berliet 4×4 lorries. The drivers had all been carefully chosen from 4,200 applicants. Only 100 were selected and the lucky crews were to see an amazing amount of the most rugged scenery Africa had to offer in thirty-four days of hard driving. The impressive convoy left Abidjan on the Ivory Coast on 29 October, 1973 and first travelled north to Tunis, crossing Niger, Algeria and Tunisia. The back-up crew also consisted of 100 people: mechanics, medics, movie cameramen and stills photographers and journalists. The Berliet lorries carried fuel, water, food, spares and radio transmitters. The convoy reached Tunis on 29 November – on schedule. Much of the driving had been across trackless deserts, across the Sahara and over the Hoggar mountains. For the Tenere Desert crossing, the convoy was split into five groups, each headed by one of the Berliet lorries, itself in radio contact with an accompanying aircraft. There were no major breakdowns and all sixty cars reached Tunis on time. The 5,000-mile route was probably the toughest that any car has done in any rally.

For a while after these events Citroën even produced a handbook for those intrepid rally-ists who wished to test themselves and their 2CV to the limit. It included all the information necessary for the would-be explorer. These days there is sufficient spares back-up to make similar rallying perfectly possible.

Having seen what was possible from the tin snail, Citroën bought a disused quarry in Argenton-sur-Creuse in 1972 and prepared it for '2CV Cross' The idea was that the unmade roads would mimic some of the conditions of the major Raids but on a short and safe circuit where speed was restricted to 70kph. The safety rules included the removal of all glass in the windows, removal of rear doors and and hood; the bonnet was to remain intact although front wings could be trimmed away somewhat. Safety rules later included a rigid roll-cage and full safety kit to be worn by drivers. The events themselves resembled stock car racing but no deliberate ramming or obstruction was allowed and the event soon became a massive spectator sport with upwards of 30,000 spectators attending the French events. Soon the idea caught on elsewhere with Portugal giving it government sponsorship and the message spread to Spain, Switzerland, Austria, Italy, Belgium, Holland and even Britain.

# 9 The 2CV Today

## MAINTAINING THE 2CV

While I don't intend this section to be a definitive workshop manual, it is a good place to pass on the tips of the professionals. Any interested home mechanic will – or should – have all the necessary manuals for maintenance work.

It is important to change the oil and filter every 3,000 miles and it is also important to use the original type of oil filter such as the 'Purflux'. Air filters can be washed in petrol and re-used at 5,000-mile intervals. Eventually, after a few washings, they will need to be replaced. Spark plugs need changing at 5,000 miles, and the NGK or Eyquem

*Typical workshop scene at Garage Levallois. To the right is a late Fourgonnette van.*

*The simple deck-chair seating can be seen in this shot of an early Belgian-built 2CV.*

types are preferable. It is advisable to grease king pins at 1,000-mile intervals, at the same time as the drive shafts. While they would probably last longer without lubrication it pays to keep up a schedule and keep them regularly attended to.

The suspension cylinders or 'pots' at the side of the chassis need occasional attention to avoid the typical rusty groan of the 2CV. What is happening when the car rocks backward and forward on the road is that the coil springs inside are rubbing against the cylinder walls. This is not serious but it has been known for the cylinders to ingress water and rot from the inside out. The application of a non-mineral-based oil under the rubber boots of the tie rod and into the cylinder will cure it. Inside the cylinder are rubber components, so it is important to use non-mineral or castor oil for this. On the same area, the pivot where the tie-rod meets the swing arm can always use a little grease applied with a stiff brush. This knife edge wearing area is particularly susceptible to corrosion from its exposure to the elements.

Gearbox oil should be changed at 10,000-mile intervals while topping up should be checked every 5,000. An EP80 or 80/90 multigrade gearbox oil should be used. The filler hole is also the level, so topping up is simple. Gearboxes are sturdy but it is inadvisable to accelerate and decelerate fiercely in reverse. The deceleration can undo the gear cluster locking rings which can wreck a gearbox.

Points and the condenser should be changed at 10,000-mile intervals, but the lack of a distributor makes this all very easy. To gain access to the contact breaker box it is necessary to remove the fan. The removal of the fan fixing bolt with a long 14mm box spanner should not give any problems but the fan is often jammed fast on its taper. Place a suitable drift in the hole and tap all round in every direction. This usually dislodges it without using gear-pullers or very big hammers! Once inside the contact breaker box, cleanliness is of paramount importance. To set the engine to the correct static firing point, slide a 4mm rod through the crankcase hole – there is

*Note cut-away rear wings on this Belgian 2CV.*

only one – and it will, on turning the engine, slot into a corresponding hole in the flywheel. While the fan is removed it makes good sense to clean the oil cooler of all dirt, flies and other detritus. This small radiator is essential for the cooling of the oil and must be kept clean. Check the oil pipe unions as well. The fins on the cylinders can also get clogged and this can seriously affect their cooling. Take time to brush and clear these, too.

On the electrics side it makes sense to replace the HT leads every year at the cost of a few pounds. Tracking can occur after a few years and for peace of mind it is simpler to replace them as a matter of course.

Exhausts are cheap and simple to replace. Mild steel are recommended but in normal use they only last a couple of years. For economy and quiet running it is wise to avoid stainless sets.

The steering components are not a problem but track rod ends can wear. Luckily the 2CV versions are adjustable and greasable. Wear is betrayed by a judder in the steering when on full lock.

A smell of unburnt gases around the engine can be traced to a cylinder head leak. There is no gasket on the cylinder heads of the 2CV engine and no sealer should ever be used to cure a leak. The components are designed to be a gas-tight fit

*Bare body on chassis ready for painting. These pictures taken at Garage Levallois display the minimal structure.*

*Typical rot at the rear of the rear door opening is dealt with before ...*

*... the body is lifted into place by two men.*

metal to metal. Leaks occur when the procedure for re-torquing the heads when the engine was new was either not carried out or done incorrectly. It is a simple job to remove the head and flat down the sealing faces with smoothing paste and a spare cylinder head barrel.

Rebuilt engines are available for around £500 exchange or about £1,000 fitted, but it is not uncommon for them to last 150–200,000 miles before major repair or complete replacement is necessary.

The 2CV is one of the few cars where chassis replacement is a routine job easily and reasonably cheaply carried out. If when considering a 2CV for purchase it is noticed that the chassis has been patched or repaired it is better to look for another example. They are so numerous and cheap to buy that it makes sense to get a good one to start with. However, the chassis themselves are available new and galvanized for around £300. A complete chassis change job by a specialist will rarely cost more than £1,000. What usually happens, though, is that as the body is stripped in readiness for removal it is found there is further rot. Even then it is easy to put right and still have money left over.

From the interior point of view a set of re-upholstered seats will only cost around £200 while a new fabric hood is all of £130. Garage Levallois even produce completely rebuilt 2CVs for around £5,500 inclusive.

2CVs do rot, of course. Floors corrode at the sides and at the front of the footwell. These are available as complete sides and are very simple to replace. Lower bulkhead areas can rot, as can the rear seat-belt mounts. While at the rear it is worth checking the integrity of the inner wing suspension bump stops as these can rot, but there are no double skins to hide anything here. All of the likely corrosion areas are easy to find if you've a pair of eyes and a torch. The bonnet hinge panel is also a problem area but, again, repair panels can be let in here with no trouble. The ventilator flap rots away but is easily replaced. In general the spares situation is fantastically good and even owners of older examples should have no trouble finding the right parts.

## BUYING A 2CV

When buying it is worth noting a few pointers. 1970–75 seem to be the best build years to choose. Build quality was still high but cars had improved 12-volt electrics and the larger 435 or 602cc engines. Dollys seemed to be rather more thrown together and quality can be very poor with these. The same is the case with Dyanes, although because they are cheaper it would pay to find an almost perfect example for the same money as a medium quality 2CV. Dyanes rarely fetch more than about £1,500–£2,000. The Charleston versions of the 2CV seemed to be well put together, though. Obviously the rarer early examples command higher prices and have their own particular charms, but for an everyday car the early Seventies seems to be the best choice. Prices start at around £800 but it pays to fork out a minimum of about £1,500 for a decent example. Even at £2,000 you won't lose money as the 2CV will hold its value; the best go for around £5,500.

Amis have a particular following but here the early examples command higher prices. The Ami-8 with its smoothed out lines lacked the character of the Ami-6 and is consequently less sought-after. It is worth noting that the Break – estate – versions rot rather severely and that the saloons are more popular. For the Ami-6 £3,500 seems about the top price here while they are very popular in Holland, where prices go up to £5,500 for perfect examples.

*Critical lighting in these of-the-period pictures reveal spot weld ripples in the bonnet sides of this 1954–5 Slough 2CV. Note also, the rear doors have opening windows, the trafficators are ahead of the front doors and there is a 'Front Drive' bonnet mascot.*

*A rebuilt engine just unpacked from the crate, complete with oil-cooler.*

## THE CLUBS

### The Citroën Car Club

The Citroën Car Club celebrates its first fifty years in 1999. In 1949 it was the first Citroen car club in the world and now there are some 200 around the world which are in regular contact. The Citroën Car Club has around 3,000 members who receive a glossy 96-page magazine every month. Advertising is free to Club members. The Club has an insurance scheme through a broker who knows the cars and caters for the classic and historic as well as the modern. Club-affiliated RAC membership offers a 15 per cent discount off the normal fee. Two club shops offer members just about everything that is available relative to the double chevron marque: clothing, badges, books and models. There is a National Rally each year attended by some 1,000 Citroëns of all ages and types and three large regional rallies in Scotland, Yorkshire and the Midlands from May to September. There are also rallies and meetings arranged by the sections throughout the year. It has always been the policy of the Citroën Car Club to welcome all

# 2CVGB

At the formation of the 2CV Club of Great Britain in February 1978 the 2CV6 had been imported officially for three and a half years, the Dyane had been on sale for almost ten years, the Ami had not long ceased to be sold and abroad the Acadiane had recently replaced the AKS400 van. As well as recent models (at this time a new 2CV6 cost £1,799 and a Dyane £1,989!) Club members owned a variety of early or imported examples such as Ami-6, Méhari, Bijou, 2CV4, 250/350/400 vans and even the odd pre-1970 2CV and so the formation of the Club neatly brought together all these different types and their no doubt equally different owners, something which still happens today.

Citroën was rather keen to sell its small but unconventional cars at this time, even if it did not really understand the sort of market which it was supplying (or perhaps even creating) and so the Club began by having a reasonable relationship with the manufacturer, in part probably due to their then-press officer being something of an enthusiast himself. However, this did not mean the Club fell into the trap of becoming a semi-official public relations organization and so as Citroën chose to distance itself from the A models, at first by indifference and latterly by more definite means, the gulf unfortunately widened, passing via the disgraceful episode of the Specials' roofs which kept flying off while the vehicles were in motion to the 'Save the 2CV' protest and the closure of the Levallois works.

The lack of enthusiasm of the maker and the dealer network for its ever more popular small cars meant that in parallel with the Club there grew a number of independent specialists. However, quite the reverse happened in the case of 2CV Cross, which was functioning strongly in Britain up to the time of the Club's foundation but which began to flounder rather badly after Citroën inexplicably withdrew its support. This was a great shame as a number of our early meetings were held in conjunction with Cross events but vehicle racing did soldier on for a number of years although it was never the same without sponsorship and foreign participation, although perhaps a new era of competition is about to dawn with the plans for 2CV circuit racing, and for many years 2CVs have been active in trials events.

'Competition' in A-model terms has really been more a case of pitting our apparently anachronistic cars against adverse conditions rather than one another and throughout the history of the Club there have always been people within the membership ready to do just that. Driving from Land's End to John O'Groats, West across North America, South into the Sahara Desert, North into the Arctic Circle and East to the furthest reaches of Europe and well beyond. Travelling in a rather less adventurous way has also been one of the most popular activities enjoyed by members and foreign meetings have had 2CVGB participation from the time that the Club was formed – for instance, some twenty-five 2CVGB cars attended the Dutch Waggel meeting just after the first issue of 2CVGB *News* was published.

Being a source of information on world-wide 2CV events has always been one of the strongest functions of 2CVGB *News*, and indeed many of the earlier issues had much of their twelve pages taken up with such notices. Our magazine has certainly passed through various stages of thickness, content, legibility and typography over the past ten years, although the format has remained basically unchanged, giving each issue a stimulating degree of unpredictability. The range of subjects so far covered is wide enough to defy description and it is heartening that so many members have taken the trouble to share their thoughts of whatever nature.

While the magazine has been the important thread running through the history of the Club the actual business of meeting one another face to face sprung logically from it with the formation of local groups, and from these that most characteristic 2CVGB activity, camping weekends. In the early days these could be enjoyed for as little as 40p per unit per night and having organized its first annual International meeting only six months after its formation the Club eventually rose to the heights of presenting a very successful World Meeting of 2CV Friends.

---

**2CVGB** (*continued*)

The foregoing was written by Martin Broadribb in 1988 and the information still holds good. My years of working as Clubs Editor on *Classic Cars* magazine gave me the opportunity to look at almost every club magazine from almost every club in the country. *2CVGB News* is an A5-sized monthly and gives a great deal of information. The magazine is often all that some

members may see of the Club, so it has to be good. From the Club's website there is access to worldwide 2CV clubs and Citroën-related subjects. I would need another book to print it all out! Take a look.

2CVGB can be contacted at PO Box 602, Crick, Northampton NN6 7UW, with email enquiries to enquiries@2cvgb.com. Web: www.2cvgb.co.uk.

---

Citroën enthusiasts, whatever model of car they own.

The Club maintains a list of 300 service and spares suppliers.

The Club can be contacted at PO Box 348, Steyning, Sussex BN44 3XN.

Web: www.citroencarclub.org.uk

## The Citroën Model & Memorabilia Club

The Citroën Model & Memorabilia Club was started in 1993 by two enthusiastic collectors in order to keep other collectors informed about the models of Citroëns that had been made in the past eighty years and to detail and describe new models as they became available. Over the years a database of more than 6,000 Citroën models has been compiled. Members of the Club receive a newsletter at regular intervals which gives information and descriptions of new models, and an extract from the database which builds up into a complete listing. The subscription is £8 for four issues, including postage in Europe.

The Club can be contacted by telephone on 0181 978 3533 or at Conwaycv2@bigfoot.com.

## 2CV SPECIALISTS

*2CV City*
Unit 8, Mearclough Mill
Mearclough Road
Sowerby Bridge
Halifax HX6 3LF
Tel: 01422 316366
Mobile: 0771 412 5459
Web: www.2cvcity.co.uk
Rebuilds, cars, spares.

*2CV Heaven*
Unit 2, 91 Western Road
Brighton
East Sussex BN1 2NW
Web: www.2cvheaven.com
Rebuilds, specials, parts, history.

*Duckcenter*
Web: www.duckcenter.com
Parts for post 1970 2CVs.

*ECAS 2CV Parts*
Unit 9, Ladford Covert Industrial Park
Seighford
Stafford ST18 9QL
Tel: 01785 282882
Fax: 01785 282883
Web: www.2cvparts.co.uk

German, Swedish, and French Car
Parts Ltd.
The Planet Centre
Armadale Road
Feltham
Middlesex TW14 0LW
Tel: 0208 917 3970
Fax: 0208 917 3982
Web: www.gsfcarparts.com

Kent Citroën
Unit 1A, Vicarage Lane
Hoo Marina, Hoo
Rochester
Kent ME3 9LB
Tel: 01634 252987
Mobile: 0860 276806
Web: www.sillycvs.co.uk
Rebuilds and spares.

## Racing Clubs

*2CV Racing Club*
6 Blackthorn Grove
Shawbirch
Telford
Shropshire TF5 0LL
Fax: 01952 253442
E-mail: info@2cvracing.co.uk
Web: www.2cvracing.co.uk

*BARC – British Automobile Racing Club Ltd*
Thruxton Circuit
Thruxton
Andover
Hampshire SP11 8PN
Tel: 01264 882200
Fax: 01264 882233
Web: www.barc.net

# Epilogue

Ploughing through swathes of material in the research for this book took me alongside the writings of journalists reporting on the 2CV when it was new. Some of the reports damned the 2CV by faint praise but others were staggered at the little car's capabilities. My wanderings also took me past the derisive comments of present day journalists busy writing about super exotic sports cars, and others who have nothing but praise for the little tin snail. Whatever the opinions and whatever the course of the discussions the 2CV shines through any arguments as a paragon of economy, practicality, charm and – buzzword of this book – exiguity (meaning scant or meagre and in Latin *exiguus* from *exigere*, to weigh exactly), something to which Pierre Boulanger and his crew were no strangers.

The 2CV could in itself be a cure for aggressive and dangerously fast driving. Take the average aggressor in a BMW, Volvo or Audi: he or she should be banned from driving you say. But no. The cure would be to confiscate the car which seems to be causing all the trouble and to hand over a standard 2CV. They must then be obliged by law to drive only that for a year. The fact that the 2CV has minimal performance and top speed but will nevertheless deliver efficient transportation, may be just the humbling experience that the road terrorist needs. Perhaps a year of driving a 2CV could at least teach respect. On the other hand it could form a deep-seated resentment over the year, which

would explode in a cataclysm of road rage when the fast car was returned.

Whatever you think of this plan, one thing is for sure: the 2CV driver has nothing to prove. As your own 2CV is overtaken by a blur of red paint, fat exhaust pipes and with an engine note all but drowned out by beating music, you might reflect on that point. The coolest hero in the George Lucas film *American Graffiti* was Curt Henderson – played by a young Richard Dreyfuss – who drove a well-used 1962 vintage 2CV, a car totally unsuited, both pragmatically and aesthetically to the American way of life. For a start it was frugal with petrol, which is something the average American is afraid of promoting. If petrol in 1999 America – in some states at least, if not in California – is available at an unbelievable 70 cents a gallon (18.5 cents a litre), it would have cost around 40 cents (10.5 cents a litre) in 1962. Curt Henderson could have travelled the 400 miles (650km) from Los Angeles to San Francisco (eventually) for around ten bucks. Try doing that in a Chevrolet Bel-Air for ten dollars! While America has never been interested in exiguity, there have at least been a few movie heroes who didn't drive fast gas-guzzlers.

James Bond usually drove Aston Martins, Lotuses and the like, but every now and then he had to use any transportation he could get. In *For Your Eyes Only* Bond escapes in a bright yellow 2CV6 and exercises the car's capabilities in true Bond fashion. Citroën were quick to cash in on the publicity by releasing 300 limited edition cars with 007 decals and fake bullet holes. Sadly they were standard 2CVs under the skin rather than the 1,015cc GS-engined examples used in the film. Before this there were appearances in which 2CVs were driven by such French stars as Brigitte Bardot, Jean Moreau and Jean-Paul Belmondo in those seminal black and white films of the 1960s and 1970s.

I recently took a trip to the Henry Doubleday Research Association's Ryton Organic Gardens. The HDRA promotes organic horticulture and has a heritage seed library and various events to promote the attitude of healthy gardening without polluting chemicals. While I took my own gas-guzzler (1954 Rover 90, 25mpg, disgraceful!) to the event, I noticed the car park had more than a handful of 2CVs in it, proving that those who wish to make less of an impact on the soil by doing their gardening without chemicals, are also enthusiastic to make the smallest impact on air quality by driving the eminently sensible 2CV.

While a drive through London reveals several 2CVs, the marque was outsold by the Renault 4. Yet where are they? Renault 4s are a very rare sight. Did they fare less well in the English weather? Were they less *de rigeur* than the 2CV? Well yes, they were so there's the answer. Fashion is everything and the 2CV is still a car to be respected on the dreariest London street or on the fanciest, sun-drenched St Tropez boulevard. Who could mistake the unique noise of that air-cooled two cylinder steadily increasing in revs as the tin snail smoothly accelerates down the road?

Most owners are fiercely enthusiastic about their 2CVs in a parental way. They forgive the little car its lack of performance because it has such charm and steadfast loyalty to the owner who spends just a little time on maintenance.

The charm of the 2CV is apparent from the archaic details which survived right up until the latest examples. The adjustable headlights – essential for the type of suspension employed – were still adjusted by the rubber handle under the dash and the wooden 'scotch' is still in place in the spare wheel well. An owner I met recently wasn't aware that the wooden scotch was a specific item in the 2CVs toolkit. She just thought it was a piece of wood. But it is cunningly designed to fit the curvature of the wheel circumference and prevent rolling when wheels are changed. There it still was alongside the spare wheel and almost unused.

Looking at modern cars today one could be forgiven for thinking that modern industry is more aware of environmental impact than it was forty years ago. Yet here are cars which use a fantastic amount of petro-chemically derived materials, such as plastics and fabrics, in the manufacture of cars, and yet the industry is employing fewer and fewer workers in an escalating search for more profit. Incredibly the average family car returns little better than 30mpg yet the technology to produce better economy has been around for decades. Why aren't we making cars which are economical on fuel? In the USA there was the beginnings of a fuel conscious change in the motor industry. Cars became smaller and less thirsty for a time, but then the whole industry was swamped with 'leisure vehicles' – usually four-wheel-drive vehicles of very robust build and employing large powerful engines. And they are used to take the kids to school and sit in traffic jams all day. The result is an average fuel consumption of 15mpg.

Look around at a typical British traffic jam. What do you see but a huge percentage of four wheel drive vehicles with not a scrap of mud on them. Taking the kids to school or driving around the city on perfectly metalled roads. The result again is an average fuel consumption of 15mpg.

At least Citroën tried to change things. Naturally it wanted to make a profit from the exercise and indeed did but eventually the bean counters at the top, aware, amongst other factors, that the petrol companies were not interested in fuel economy, decided to shelve the 2CV as an embarrassing oddity in Citroën's history. The company today is not remotely interested in the appearance of this new book about the 2CV. It is a sad thing that a modern company does not champion the fine designs of its own past. BMW's Mobile Tradition recognizes the importance of its own past and positively promotes interest in and maintenance of old BMWs. It believes, quite rightly that someone who is helped to run and keep a classic BMW will also be very likely to own a new BMW too. Many similar companies could take a leaf out of that book.

Boulanger and his team gave the world a fine motor car in the 2CV, and gave the world his recognition that small was beautiful, economy important and supercar performance unnecessary. My job has been simply to illustrate that fine philosophy and bring the story, to the best of my ability, on to the bookshelf.

# Appendix I
# Annual Production of 2CV Types 1949–90

| Year | 2CV Saloon | 2CV Van | 2CV 4×4 | Dyane Saloon | Acadiane | Méhari | FAF & Baby-B | Total |
|---|---|---|---|---|---|---|---|---|
| 1949 | 876 | | | | | | | 876 |
| 1950 | 6,196 | | | | | | | 6,196 |
| 1951 | 14,592 | 1,696 | | | | | | 16,288 |
| 1952 | 21,124 | 7,711 | | | | | | 28,835 |
| 1953 | 35,361 | 13,121 | | | | | | 48,482 |
| 1954 | 52,791 | 19,197 | | | | | | 71,988 |
| 1955 | 81,170 | 23,904 | | | | | | 105,074 |
| 1956 | 95,864 | 23,859 | | | | | | 119,723 |
| 1957 | 107,250 | 31,431 | | | | | | 138,681 |
| 1958 | 126,332 | 37,631 | | | | | | 163,963 |
| 1959 | 145,973 | 50,058 | | | | | | 196,031 |
| 1960 | 152,801 | 57,724 | 20 | | | | | 210,545 |
| 1961 | 158,659 | 56,639 | 274 | | | | | 215,572 |
| 1962 | 144,759 | 54,191 | 112 | | | | | 199,062 |
| 1963 | 158,035 | 55,775 | 87 | | | | | 213,897 |
| 1964 | 167,419 | 64,994 | 138 | | | | | 232,551 |
| 1965 | 154,023 | 59,211 | 35 | | | | | 213,269 |
| 1966 | 168,357 | 55,817 | 27 | | | | | 224,201 |
| 1967 | 98,683 | 55,281 | | 47,712 | | | | 201,676 |
| 1968 | 57,473 | 51,545 | | 98,769 | | 837 | 495 | 209,119 |
| 1969 | 72,044 | 53,259 | | 95,434 | | 12,624 | 300 | 233,661 |

*(continued overleaf)*

*Appendix I: Annual Production of 2CV Types 1949–90*

| Year | 2CV Saloon | 2CV Van | 2CV 4×4 | Dyane Saloon | Acadiane | Méhari | FAF & Baby-B | Total |
|------|-----------|---------|---------|--------------|----------|--------|--------------|-------|
| 1970 | 121,096 | 46,485 | | 96,456 | | 11,246 | 660 | 275,943 |
| 1971 | 121,264 | 62,074 | 1 | 97,091 | | 10,175 | 2,430 | 293,035 |
| 1972 | 133,530 | 64,592 | | 111,462 | | 11,742 | 2,025 | 323,351 |
| 1973 | 123,819 | 68,357 | | 95,535 | | 12,567 | 1,125 | 301,403 |
| 1974 | 163,143 | 64,325 | | 126,854 | | 13,910 | 2,280 | 370,512 |
| 1975 | 122,542 | 44,821 | | 117,913 | | 8,920 | 4,050 | 298,246 |
| 1976 | 134,396 | 54,533 | | 118,871 | | 9,569 | 1,290 | 318,659 |
| 1977 | 132,458 | 52,721 | | 113,474 | 141 | 9,645 | 2,010 | 310,449 |
| 1978 | 108,825 | 12,647 | | 102,958 | 37,787 | 8,467 | 3,390 | 274,074 |
| 1979 | 101,222 | 2,535 | | 77,605 | 49,679 | 8,995 | 5,070 | 245,106 |
| 1980 | 89,994 | 135 | | 61,745 | 45,438 | 8,351 | 3,510 | 209,173 |
| 1981 | 89,472 | 30 | | 39,176 | 30,881 | 4,833 | 2,295 | 166,687 |
| 1982 | 86,060 | | | 27,960 | 36,054 | 4,137 | 1,590 | 155,801 |
| 1983 | 59,673 | | | 13,908 | 20,377 | 3,349 | 600 | 97,907 |
| 1984 | 54,923 | | | 570 | 12,756 | 2,654 | | 70,903 |
| 1985 | 54,067 | | | | 8,429 | 1,882 | 30 | 64,408 |
| 1986 | 56,663 | | | | 7,915 | 669 | | 65,247 |
| 1987 | 43,255 | | | | 3,936 | 381 | 30 | 47,602 |
| 1988 | 22,717 | | | | | | | 22,717 |
| 1989 | 19,077 | | | | | | | 19,077 |
| 1990 | 9,954 | | | | | | | 9,954 |
| **Totals** | *3,867,932* | *1,246,299* | *694* | *1,443,493* | *253,393* | *144,953* | *33,180* | *6,989,944* |

# Appendix II
# 2CV Models

David Conway has helped me compile this section, providing models for photography and writing the brief history of scale model production of the Citroën 2CV. He is early 2CV officer of the Citroën Car Club and runs the Models Collector's Club

From the start of the car manufacturing company in 1919, André Citroën was aware of the need to make the name Citroën known and recognized. One of his lesser-known publicity projects was the manufacture of models of his cars under the name *Jouets Citroën*. These were probably the first models to be made that were reasonably accurate representations of the full-size cars that were sold. His doctrine was that a child's first words should be 'Mama', 'Papa' and 'Citroën'. His original 'toys' were made in tinplate and would not pass the regulations for toys laid down nowadays. In addition, they are now worth many hundreds of pounds. Eighty years on, toy cars have become models and are bought more by adults than by children. It seems that nearly every owner of a car a little bit away from the run of the mill will have a miniature somewhere around his house or office. The 2CV driver will probably have several models of his pride and joy and the industry has given him a wide choice.

By the time the 2CV was launched in 1948, the manufacture of Citroën toys or models by the parent company had ceased but production of toy cars or models was now world-wide, although the principal

*The first models of the 2CV were made in 1950, appropriately enough by JRD which was the company which carried on the production in tinplate of the original* Jouets Citroën. *Note the clockwork motor and the large boot which was a non-standard accessory at the time.*

base was still in Europe. The models were now smaller and mostly made in metal alloy or plastics, although some factories – such as JRD, who had taken over the production of the original *Jouets Citroën* – still made models in tinplate.

The first model of the 2CV did not appear on sale until two years after the launch of the car. Perhaps they were waiting to see if the car was really a commercial success. In fact it was JRD, the company which had carried on the tradition of the *Jouets Citroën*, which produced the first model of the 2CV in 1950. This was, like the first *Jouets*

*Dinky (France). The first version of the 2CV produced in 1952.*

*Citroën*, a tinplate model, but in 1:25 scale. The later JRD tinplate models were made in the larger 1:20 scale which was more common in the industry.

It was not until two years later in 1952 that the first Dinky Toy model of the 2CV came on the market from the French branch of the Meccano Company. This was given the reference number 24T and was the only model in the series which was not sold individually boxed in the traditional yellow carton. There were a number of changes made to the model in the course of its nine-year production, but for the collector interested in minor casting differences, different wheels and different colours, the information is available elsewhere. One change to the model which followed a change to the car was the fitting of three lights to the rear instead of the original single light in the centre of the number plate. A 1:40 scale model in Zamac, which is an aluminium alloy known also as Mazak, was introduced by JRD in 1956 and a 1:48 simple model in plastic was introduced by Clement Gaget by his company 'Cle' in 1954 and remained in production in various guises and in different scales for nearly twenty years.

At the last count there were more than a thousand models of the 2CV on the database kept by the Citroën Model & Memorabilia Collectors Club. There have been models in sizes from 1:3 – the electric children's car from TT Toys – to 1:220 made in resin by Adam. This list does not include models with only minor variations which would only be of interest to the fanatic or obsessive 'rivet counter'. However, there are still a sufficient number of different models to be of interest to the car enthusiast as well as the model enthusiast.

For the 2CV driver who is looking for a model of his own car the market is well supplied. Norev made the change from making toys that were collected as models to making models for collectors in 1993. The relatively new Portuguese company, Vitesse, added the 2CV to their range in 1990. Both companies have produced series of models on a year-by-year basis with the models showing the changes, minor or major, made to the real car from the first 1948 version to the latest production versions. The Vitesse range covers most years through to the 1982 Charleston. Norev continues through to the Dolly. Both companies have made models of the various special editions such as the Sahara, Spot, the France 3/Beachcomber and the James Bond 007 car. Norev has concentrated its production on models of production cars, whereas Vitesse has made more limited editions and promotional items. The other principal difference between the two ranges is that Vitesse are die-cast metal, while Norev are made in a resin/plastics material allied to a metal chassis. There are many collectors who still insist on having only models made in metal (perhaps a carry-over from their childhood playing with the original Dinky Toys on the floor), but the use of modern materials does help the manufacturer to include much more detail in a product which is made for exhibition rather than play.

*CLE (Clement Gaget) plastic 2CV Van in 1:32, 1:48 and 1:64 scale, 1954–62.*

The lines of the 2CV changed very little in the course of its production run and are instantly recognizable. However, there have been a number of variations to the basic shape, most of which have been made in model form. The most common is the van which was seen all over France and neighbouring countries for many years and is now kept on the road by enthusiasts. Like the car, there have been changes to the van over the years. The type of bonnet and the presence or absence of windows are the most obvious differences. Models of the van have been made by most of the model manufacturers which produced the saloons, Norev, Dinky, JRD and Cle being the most prolific. There is of course the possibility of a greater number of variations on a van model as various liveries and colours can be used. In its most simple form, the company name can be displayed on the side in the form of a paper label as was used on the first Norev models, or as a waterslide transfer or, as is most widely used now, a tampo print which is also called a pad print and is as permanent as the paint. JRD models were reissued from 1987 but could be distinguished from the first series as they had different base plates and there were new liveries on the vans. A number of vans were issued by the new Norev company, but some of the original tooling went to Eligor which produced the later van with the windows in the sides.

There has always been a demand from the car enthusiast as well as the collector for the unusual and historic. Although the basic 2CV car and van were produced by many different manufacturers, models of the prototypes were not made until 1982 when Idem

*This simple tinplate and plastic Van was made by Sesame from 1960–75. It was produced as one of a series of low-priced toys to sell at FF1 although it would probably not meet the latest CE regulations for toys. In addition to the six or seven versions sold to the toy trade many others were produced in liveries for commercial companies, but these are extremely rare.*

185

made a white metal kit of the 1939 prototype and in 1983 when Oldies made a resin kit of the pick-up prototype. OKC also made a very crude white metal kit of the UK market pick-up, and Heco made a very good model but with one error as a result of copying a photograph rather than the actual vehicle: the four small lumps on the front wing were the rubber feet from a roof rack left there when Stuart Watkins' car was photographed for the book by Bob MacQueen.

In 1991 Norev produced a very detailed model of the 1939 prototype to be followed by models of the prototype pick-up and another three versions that had not previously been modelled. It followed these with models of the 1957 Dagonet, the 1953 Barbot 'Yacco' special and a pick-up in various liveries. The missing 2CV cars with special bodies such as the Bijou and the Umap and some of the racing versions have been made by Ministyle, and even such unusual vehicles as the Iranian Méhari have been made as a model for the collector.

Although the majority of the model-makers concentrated on the 2CV car and van, the other A series derivatives have not been ignored. The Dyane has been made by Corgi, Dinky and Norev, and the Ami-6 and Ami-8 in both saloon and estate versions have been made by Solido, Norev, Dinky, Corgi and Eligor, among others. The Méhari was originally made in 1:10 scale by Vullierme as a promotional model for the Citroën Company and later by Polistil, Minialuxe and Norev; the later productions from Norev are the best reproductions.

Although the production of the 2CV car has ceased, production of the models continues. Manufacturers find new versions to make such as the Snowplough 2CV from Vitesse, which was shown in the catalogue as 'sold out' before it appeared in the shops, or they reissue old versions such as the James Bond 2CV from Corgi which also appeared as a limited edition.

*The Méhari was made by Norev in various colours from 1970–88 in plastic (ref. 137). It was reintroduced in 1993 with more detail and with a greater number of colour versions (ref. 150901).*

*The 2CV has been modelled in many materials, including leather as in this version made in France.*

*Crystal de Paris is one of the firms which has made models of the 2CV in glass to a very high standard.*

*Polistil made models of the 2CV in 1:25 scale from 1977–90. The 2CV Cross version was available in blue, white or orange (ref. S.700).*

## MANUFACTURERS OF 2CV MODELS

At the time of writing the following are the principal manufacturers making models of the 2CV and its derivatives. All are 1:43 except where specified. There are other specialist firms and individuals whose production is intermittent.

*The gaily painted ceramic 2CVs are made in Columbia and range in size from 9–40cm in length.*

Vitesse: 2CV saloon in numerous versions, priced around £16. Obtainable from most model shops.

Solido: 2CV Saloon 1:17 and 1:43, priced around £18 and £8, respectively. Obtainable from most model shops.

Norev: 2CV Saloon, van, pick-up and prototypes, priced from £18 to £47. Obtainable from Citroën Model & Memorabilia Collectors Club (CMMCC) and model shops in France.

Herpa: 2CV Saloon 1:87, priced around £5. Obtainable from model railway specialists.

Eligor: 2CV Van and Ami-6, priced around £14. Obtainable from a few specialist model shops and from the CMMCC.

Original Miniatures: kits and handbuilt models of Ami-6 Break, Dyane etc, priced around £32 for kits and £92 for handbuilt models. Obtainable from a few specialist model shops and from the CMMCC.

Columbian Ceramic: decorated cars in sizes from 9cm to 40cm, priced from £5 to £150. Obtainable from the CMMCC.

This list is not comprehensive: for information on other models of the 2CV contact the Citroën Model & Memorabilia Collectors Club, tel/fax: 0118 978 3533.

## WHAT IS IT WORTH? WILL IT INCREASE IN VALUE IF I KEEP IT?

These are the questions that most collectors do not want to be asked. The answer to the second question is probably more easily given than the answer to the first. A fair answer is that it depends on what it is and when it was

*The Solido 2CV in 1:17 scale (ref. 8028) has been made since 1994 in various colours and versions. The model shown is one of the few made by the factory with a limited production run. Only 500 were made in this livery, to promote a toy fair in Belgium in 1994.*

made. The answer will almost certainly be no if the model has been made in the past thirty years. If it was made before 1939, the answer will depend on when it was bought and how much was paid for it. The true collector will buy because he likes and wants the particular model in his collection. If it is bought with a view to profit, it is bought by an investor or dealer, not by a collector.

However, most collectors can be excused for wishing to know the value of their collection, even if only for insurance purposes, and for that reason price guides are produced from time to time. They are always criticized for being inaccurate, incomplete and out of touch with the market, but they are only called 'guides'.

The following figures for a few of the more interesting, rare and valuable models are given for interest and are liable to be 100 per cent inaccurate. They are taken from the Argus guide of 1995 and are for models in perfect original condition in a perfect box. They do, however, show the variation that is possible.

The highest valuation given is for a Dinky Toy van of 1968 advertising 'Pirelli' with the reference number 560E, which is shown as being worth £1,800! The standard red van of the series (Ref 25d or 562) is listed at £40. The first Dinky car is listed at £60 and the first JRD Tinplate models are shown at about £200, but some of the vans with the rarer advertising are listed at more than £400. There is a gold-painted version of the James Bond 2CV by Corgi which is listed at £85. The Spanish firm Pilen made copies of Dinky which are listed as being worth around £30.

## WHAT SHALL I COLLECT?

If you want a selection of accurate models of the different versions of the 2CV, look for the current models from Vitesse and Norev. Most of the different versions produced over the years have been made by these two companies. If you want models of the Ami and Dyane, you will have to look at the range from Eligor and some of the manufacturers of kits. These are not likely to appreciate in value, but as a result of modern technology the models are more detailed and usually more accurate than the older ones. However, old toys have a charm of their own and are probably more likely to appreciate in value.

*Toys Toys (Italy) Charleston pedal car in burgundy. 1989.*

# Bibliography

Borgé & Viasnoff, *La 2CV* (Ballard, 1977)

MacQueen and McNamara, *Life and Times of the 2CV* (Great Ouse Press, 1982)

Taylor, *The Citroën 2CV & Derivatives* (Motor Racing Publications, 1983)

Jacobs, *Citroën 2CV* (Osprey, 1989)

Sabates, *Album 2CV* (Editions EPA, 1992)

Sparrow, *Citroën 2CV* (Veloce, 1992)

Jacques Wolgensinger, *La 2CV* (Gallinard, 1995)

Reynolds, *Sixty Years of the Citroën 2CV* (Sutton, 1997)

# Index

The Citroën 2CV is one of the truly great car designs of all time. Conceived in the 1930s as a cheap car capable of carrying two people and fifty kilos of potatoes at a speed of 60km/h, it had also to be very economical and able to withstand the punishment meted out by the rural roads of France.

The car was unveiled in 1948 and remained in production until 1990. Popular both within and outside its native France, the *Deux Chevaux* found favour among the rural classes and chic city-dwellers, and it has become one of the motoring icons of the twentieth century.

Matt White has researched the full story of this fascinating people's car, including the Ami, Dyane and commercial variants. This fully illustrated title will be vital reading matter for all fans of the 'Tin Snail'.

- Full specifications
- The 2CV in motor sport
- Illustrated in black and white and colour
- British-made 2CVs

**For details of our other books visit www.crowood.com**

Cover design by Maggie Mellett

ISBN 1-86126-731-2

£14.99

$24.95 US

9 781861 267313